INCLUDES
DVD
VIDEO

SPRAY
FINISHING
MADE SIMPLE

JEFF JEWITT

The Taunton Press

The Taunton Press

The Taunton Press, Inc., 63 South Main Street, PO Box 5506, Newtown, CT 06470-5506
e-mail: tp@taunton.com

Editor: Helen Albert
Copy editor: Seth Reichgott
Indexer: Cathy Goddard
Interior design: Susan Fazekas
Layout: Sandra Mahlstedt
Illustrator: Christopher Mills
Photographer: Randy O'Rourke
DVD Producer: Helen Albert
DVD Editing: Gary Junken

Library of Congress Cataloging-in-Publication Data

Jewitt, Jeff.
  Spray finishing made simple / Jeff Jewitt.
    p. cm.
  ISBN 978-1-60085-092-9
  1. Wood finishing. 2. Spray painting. I. Title.
  TT325.J423 2010
  684.1'043--dc22

                    2009040226

Printed in the United States of America
10 9 8 7 6 5 4 3 2 1

The following manufacturers/names appearing in *Spray Finishing Made Simple* are trademarks: 3M®, Apollo®, B-I-N®, DAP®, Floetrol®, Ford®, General Finishes®, Hood® Finishing Products, Iwata®, Rockler℠ Woodworking and Hardware, SealCoat®, ScotchBrite®, Teflon®, Target Coatings®, Woodcraft®

acknowledgments

I'd like to thank the following individuals and companies who helped out in the production of this book and video.

At the Taunton Press—Helen Albert, who came up with the idea, Anatole and Robin Burkin, who "lent" me the workshop in the video, Gary Junken, whose deft hand behind a camera made my job seamless, and Randy O'Rourke, the best finishing photographer in the world. Also Mark Schofield at *Fine Woodworking* who lent time and materials for the video. Thanks to you all.

Also, Jeff Weiss at Target Coatings and Tom Monahan at General Finishes, who provided time, advice, and waterborne finishing products. At Wagner Spray Tech, Steve Machacek, and at 3M/Accuspray, Scott Noll for his support and help.

Finally, my ever patient wife Susan, who always helps on photography and keeps everything flowing smoothly while I'm writing books and shooting videos.

contents

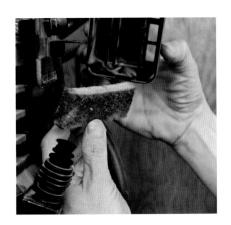

Where to
spray

One of the most important decisions you'll need to make before you begin spraying is where you can set up your spray equipment. This is important not only from a safety perspective, but also for quality of the result. Where you spray and how well you exhaust the overspray you produce will determine how good a finish you'll get.

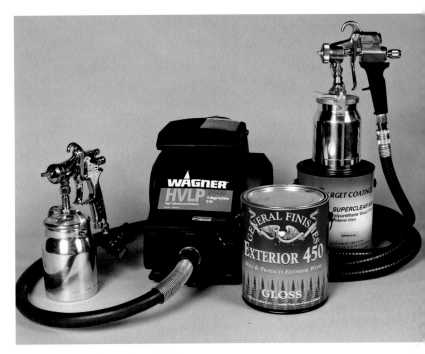

HVLP systems and waterborne finishes are a great combination for homeowners who want to spray safely at home.

A range of choices

For a home shop, there are several areas to spray safely and efficiently, depending on the type of space you have to do your woodworking. If you only spray occasionally, there are some temporary areas to set up that can be taken down easily later. We'll also look at areas that you can dedicate to spraying if you do it on a more frequent basis. In this chapter we'll look at the most practical areas for spraying and how to equip the spaces properly.

In the past, small shop woodworkers who wanted to spray had to work outside because of the large amount of flammable overspray thrown off by high-pressure spray equipment. Today home woodworkers can take advantage of two recent developments in finishing products and materials to safely spray at home; HVLP (high volume, low pressure) spray equipment and vastly improved waterborne finishing materials. HVLP equipment significantly reduces overspray. Waterborne finishes eliminate the danger of fire and greatly reduce the odor typical of solvent based finishes.

Because of these developments, you can safely spray outside, in a garage, in a basement, or in an attached building or outbuilding. We'll look at each of these options so you can make the best choice for your situation.

Spraying outside

Spraying outside is arguably the easiest, safest, and most economical option. A large open space makes it impossible for flammable vapors, which can ignite, to build up. And your setup can be minimal. Simply set up some portable sawhorses and go to work. The main downsides, besides the limitations of good weather, are bugs and other debris blowing into the finish while it's still wet. You can get around this to some degree by constructing a plastic "tent" in which to spray.

You'll need to spray in a temperature range of 60°F to 80°F and avoid humidity over 75 percent. Always spray in a shaded area like the back of a building.

Spraying inside

When you spray outdoors, the overspray (the part of the atomized finish that doesn't land on your project) simply goes up into the air. If you try to spray indoors and expect that the overspray will simply go out an open window or door, you'll quickly find that it won't. Ideally, when spraying indoors you should work in an enclosed space (we'll refer to this as a "booth").

As long as the weather cooperates, the simplest place to spray is outside.

A booth confines the overspray so it can be exhausted via a fan run by an electric motor. This exhaust can be through a window, a door, or in the case of a garage, the overhead door. The booth can be constructed of lightweight building materials like rigid foam insulation or you can hang plastic sheets or tarps from the ceiling which can be rolled up when not in use. The fan you use should be sized to the opening you have, and if you are spraying flammable finishes, should be rated as "explosion proof." Because of the high cost of these fans, you may want to spray only waterborne products when working inside. With waterborne finishes you can use an inexpensive box fan or choose something more permanent, like an industrial shutter-mount fan. Here are some basic ideas for spray areas inside.

Because this mandolin maker doesn't finish large pieces of furniture, his booth is simply an explosion-proof fan behind a table. Note the funneled sides of the booth are painted white to improve visibility.

Garages

A garage is a great place to spray because of its large open design. Depending on your available space you can make a dedicated booth or a temporary one. For a dedicated booth, choose a location that will make it easy to exhaust the overspray. If you have a window large enough to accommodate a fan, that's your best choice. The booth should be large enough to fit the projects that you make. Resist the urge to make the booth too large because it decreases the efficiency of the fan.

When the booth is in use, you should open an outside door or the overhead door a bit to let in fresh air. Many times you can simply arrange your work in front of the overhead door and then put a floor fan behind you to push the overspray out the door. Unfortunately this doesn't work when the wind is blowing through the door, so you may want to invest a little money in a knockdown, temporary garage booth (see pp. 10–11).

Basements

Basements are not ideal for spray finishing. Heaters and other appliances may spark when starting, so you cannot spray flammable finishes. Basements are often dark and don't have windows large enough to accommodate fans.

Either window in this unattached garage could hold an exhaust fan, but the one on the left is a better choice. It's lower and the window can easily be closed when the fan is not in use.

If you do spray in a basement, use only waterborne finishes. Put an exhaust fan in one window in or near your spray area and open another window to let in fresh air. If this isn't possible, you can simply put a fan behind your spray area and blow the overspray toward an open window. If you don't have a spray booth, make sure to put drop cloths over nearby items, such as tools and equipment, to avoid coating them with overspray.

Attached or outbuilding

If you're lucky enough to have a separate building for your shop, this is your best choice for spraying. Being separate from the main house helps solve the problem of residual smell from finishes. Usually, such buildings have windows that will accommodate different types of exhaust fans. (Just make sure you direct the overspray away from vehicles or neighbors who might complain of the smell.)

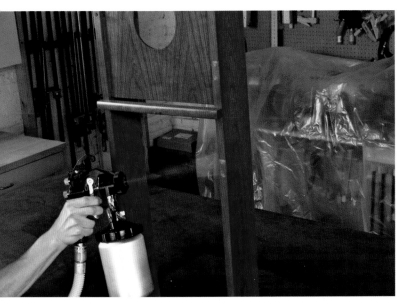

If you spray in a basement, use only waterborne finishes. When window or exhaust options are limited, just place a fan behind you to push the overspray away from the furniture. Note the plastic drop cloth to protect tools and workbenches.

workSmart

Removing overspray from tool surfaces is sticky business. It's much easier to prevent it from getting there in the first place. Cover all cast iron tables with a drop cloth.

Plastic tarps are an inexpensive way to enclose your spray area.

If the spray area is in your woodshop, you can make a temporary booth from plastic tarps that are suspended from hooks in the ceiling or joists. In the example shown here, I placed an explosion-proof fan assembly in the window and then blocked off the rest of the open window with plywood. I built a small box from MDF to hold a furnace filter in front of the fan. The plastic tarps hung from the ceiling joists complete the spray booth.

The right environment for spraying

After you've chosen where you will spray, the next step is to create the right environment for spraying. The right temperature and good light are essential to good results.

Heating

The ideal temperature for applying finishes is between 65°F to 76°F. When you exhaust overspray outside, you're also exhausting heat. There really isn't a good way around this, but from a safety standpoint you should avoid spraying flammable finishes around heaters. The best solution is bring the room to temperature, turn off the heater, spray the finish and exhaust the overspray as much as you can, then turn the heater back on so the finish can dry in a heated environment. If you're using strictly waterborne finishes, you can use the same strategy so you don't waste heat.

If you use an exhaust fan, always use a filter. Inexpensive furnace filters are the best.

Lighting

To get the best results, you must be able to see your work clearly. Ideally you should have a combination of overhead lighting and side lighting so you can see horizontal surfaces better. If you dedicate an area to a permanent or temporary booth try to locate it where there's an overhead fluorescent light fixture. Even with good overhead lighting it's hard to see some areas as you're spraying. Plan on investing in a portable halogen work light that can be focused on a specific area. Halogen work lights are inexpensive. Mounted on a tripod, they can easily be positioned where needed.

Overhead fluorescent lights are best for finishing work.

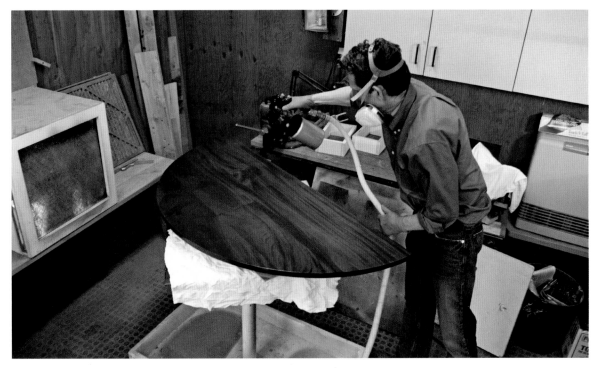

The in-the-wall heater shown at the right is propane, which could pose a serious safety hazard when spraying a flammable finish. If you do spray flammable finish, always make sure the heater is turned off. Once the overspray is evacuated you can turn it back on.

Portable halogen task lighting is a great addition to a spray booth because it can be adjusted to just about any height and angle.

Getting accurate color

If you want the most accurate color rendition, get daylight-balanced tubes for your overheard fluorescent fixtures. These reproduce colors more accurately, especially if you're trying to match a color.

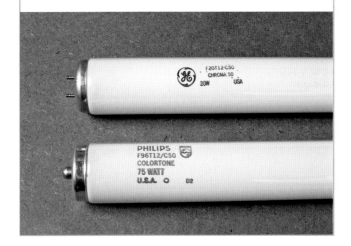

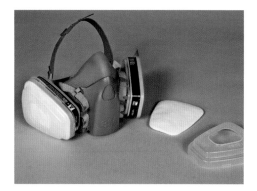

Always wear a respirator, even when spraying safer waterborne finishes.

Always have a fire extinguisher that's in good working condition. Make sure it's rated for extinguishing flammable liquids.

Safety

Every woodshop ought to have a fire extinguisher, but for spraying it must be rated for flammable liquids. Look for a fire extinguisher rated A-B-C, which means it's suitable for combustible wood and paper, flammable liquids, and electrical fires.

You should wear a respirator to protect your lungs when spraying finishes, whether solvent- or water-based. Buy a mask-style respirator that's rated for paint and organic vapors. Some stores may sell it as a paint/pesticide mask. The soft pliable mask has elastic straps that fit over your nose and mouth. Two canisters attach to the mask. Over the canisters are paper pre-filters. The paper pre-filter will remove large particles of paint and the cartridge filter inside, made from activated carbon, absorbs and removes the paint vapors.

The paper pre-filters need to be changed more often and they will load up quickly if you spray a lot of paint. Change the pre-filter when it appears dirty. Change the cartridge when you can smell finishes or solvents when wearing the mask. If you need the mask for just one job, you can get a cheaper disposable cartridge-style paint mask which is about half the cost of the re-usable ones.

Making your own spray booth

A temporary knockdown booth is fairly inexpensive to make as long as you don't have to use an explosion-proof fan. I've made several of these for friends and you can use rigid foam insulation that's very lightweight and easy to cut. A window box fan behind an opening in the center panel works as an exhaust fan.

Materials for the booth are available at your local home improvement store. Rigid foam insulation comes 1 in. or 2 in. thick. The 2-in. rigid foam is more stable and will last longer. If it's tongue and groove, cut the tongue off. Don't use foil covered insulation.

Spraying at a Business

Before you spray finish in a commercial building or on commercially zoned property, you must check with your local authorities (typically a fire marshall or equivalent). This is important, even if you're spraying non-flammable finishes. You don't want to waste money on equipment that may not pass local codes. Typically codes require a metal booth with filters and exhaust fans rated to exhaust vapors at a specific rate.

Pre-fabricated booths are available from several suppliers in many sizes to suit different requirements. Before you invest in a booth, contact a professional spray-booth designer/installer to make sure your choice will pass codes in your area.

This metal booth satisfies local ordinances.

A knockdown spray booth

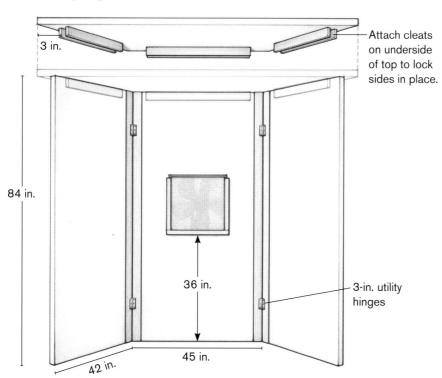

3 in.

Attach cleats on underside of top to lock sides in place.

84 in.

36 in.

3-in. utility hinges

42 in.

45 in.

Building a knockdown spray booth

1

2

3

4

5

6

This booth is easy to build, but it should only be used with waterborne finishes. The dimensions given are for a garage booth, but they can be re-sized to your requirements. Adjust as necessary to fit your own requirements. A 7-ft.-high booth should fit under most garage doors, but measure the opening to make sure and make any necessary height adjustments.

1. **Cut three of the four rigid foam sheets** to 84 in. Cut two of these sheets to 42 in. wide for the two wings. A tablesaw works best for cutting the product.

2. **Center one of the furnace filters** approximately 36 in. from the bottom of the center panel and mark an outline around it using a marker.

3. **Mark four lines** 1 in. inside this line and cut it out with a utility knife. Using the foamboard adhesive, attach 1x1 wood scraps around the two sides and bottom of the cutout for the filter holder.

4. **Attach 1½-in. wide ¼-in. plywood strips** to hold the filter in place.

5. **Attach the four 3-in. wide ¼ in. plywood strips** to the inside edges of the two wings and the two sides of the center panel using the foamboard adhesive. Allow to dry.

6. **Attach the two wings** to the center panel using the four hinges. Stand the booth upright and bring the two wings inward so it stands on its own. The wings typically are 45 degrees inward, but you can tweak this angle to your space. Lay the last piece of insulation over the top and cut it down for the top, making one edge flush with the front inward edge of the booth and leaving at least 3 in. overhang at the back and sides. Mark the top underneath where it sits on the two wings and the back panel on the outside and inside (6 lines total). Glue two strips of scrap wood on the outside of these 6 lines so the top "locks" the two wings when it's placed on top. Spray the inside of the booth white when you're done for better visibility when working in the booth. Place a window fan facing out on the outside of the center hole so it pulls air through the center.

The completed booth fits neatly inside a garage door.

Materials list
(4) 4x8 sheets of rigid foam insulation 1 in. to 2 in. thick
(4) 3-in. x 84-in. strips of plywood
(4) 3-in. utility hinges
(1) Tube foamboard adhesive
(4) 20-in. x 25-in. x 1-in. furnace filters (get the cheapest ones they have)
Scrap plywood for filter holder

Equipment

Spray equipment has come a long way from the compressor-driven, high-pressure guns of 30 years ago. Modern HVLP (high volume, low pressure) systems are user friendly for woodworking and for home improvement projects. In this chapter we'll help you choose the one for you.

Turbines and compressors

There are two broad categories of HVLP spray guns. The key difference is in the air source. In a turbine-driven HVLP spray gun, low-pressure air is produced by a blower

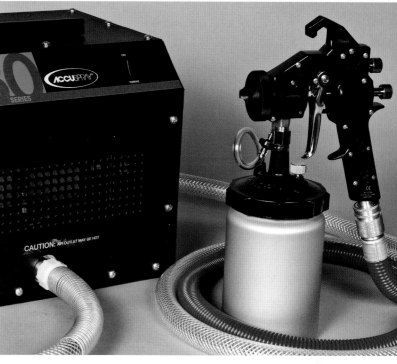

HVLP turbine systems are always sold as packages, which include a turbine unit that produces the low pressure air, an HVLP spray gun, and a hose.

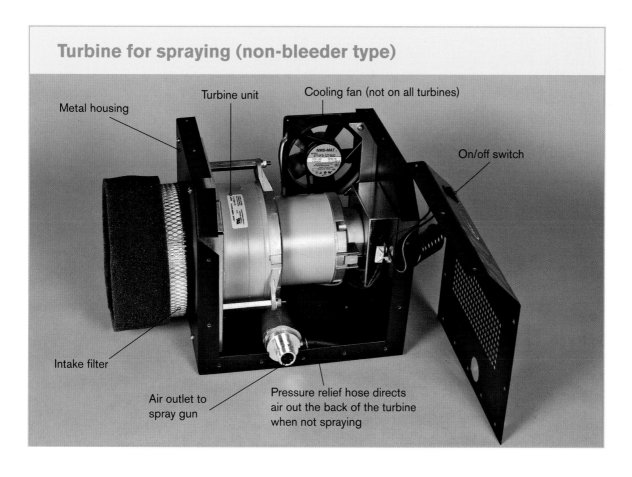

Turbine for spraying (non-bleeder type)

Metal housing

Turbine unit

Cooling fan (not on all turbines)

On/off switch

Intake filter

Air outlet to spray gun

Pressure relief hose directs air out the back of the turbine when not spraying driven by an electric motor. The turbine is constantly producing air which flows into the gun.

In a compressor-driven HVLP system, like the one shown on p. 12, air is pumped into a storage tank under high pressure, then released to operate the spray gun. The gun is connected to the compressor with an air hose and quick-disconnect fittings. Water filters are always necessary with compressed air. Since the air coming from the tank is under high pressure, it has to be decompressed (or converted) to a lower pressure for an HVLP gun. This process takes place within the gun, and this is called an HVLP conversion gun.

Turbine systems

Early turbine systems fed the constant air from the turbine blower through the front of the spray gun, whether or not you were spraying finish. These are called "bleeder" systems, because the gun is constantly pushing air

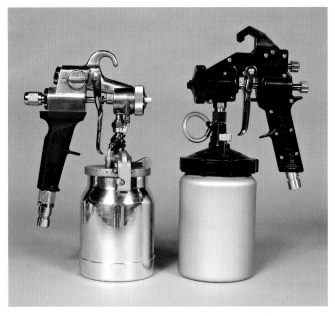

Turbine guns always have a large ¾-in. air fitting. Earlier designs were bleeder guns, but these two examples from current manufacturers are both non-bleeder guns.

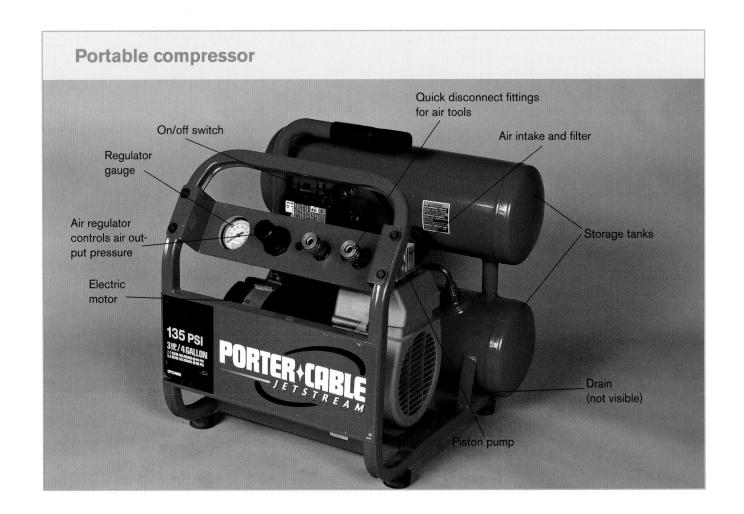

Portable compressor

On/off switch

Regulator gauge

Quick disconnect fittings for air tools

Air intake and filter

Air regulator controls air output pressure

Storage tanks

Electric motor

135 PSI
3 HP / 4 GALLON

PORTER·CABLE
JETSTREAM

Drain (not visible)

Piston pump

through the front of the gun. This was considered such a disadvantage that today most turbines are sold as "non-bleeder" systems. In this design, the air from the turbine is released only when the gun is spraying finish. Lower-cost "bleeder" turbine systems may still be purchased. Despite the annoyance of the constant air flow, it doesn't affect the quality of the finish.

When you purchase a turbine HVLP, you typically buy a complete system in which you get the turbine, the hose, and the gun. The turbine is attached to the spray gun with a large diameter hose about the width of a standard garden hose. Since turbine systems are most often sold to homeowners and hobbyists, manufacturers may include accessories like extra nozzles, a viscosity measuring cup, filters, and such.

Compressor systems

A compressor operates on stored energy. The pump pistons compress air from low to high pressure. The pressurized air is stored in a tank and then released through an air regulator. Compressors are available as one-stage or two-stage, which refers to how many times the air is compressed. Typically, single-stage compressors are used for portable compressors while two-stage compressors are found on stationary compressors. Two-stage compressors are more efficient and run cooler.

Compressed air is measured in SCFM (standard cubic feet per minute) and psi (pounds per square inch). These two values are important. They indicate the maximum amount of air the compressor can produce as well as how much air a spray gun needs to operate.

The spray gun connects to the compressor with a hose that's smaller in diameter and more lightweight than a turbine hose. You have a choice of sizes when you buy a hose, from ¼ in. to ⅜ in. ID (inside diameter). For an HVLP gun you should use ⁵⁄₁₆ in. for lengths from the gun to the compressor of 15 ft. or less, and ⅜ in. from 15 ft. to 50 ft. Try not to exceed 25 ft. if possible. Fittings called "quick-disconnects" are used with air hoses. When you remove the hose from the gun, they shut off the air. A compressor will produce air containing water (especially

Though they are different sizes, either of these compressors will operate an HVLP spray gun.

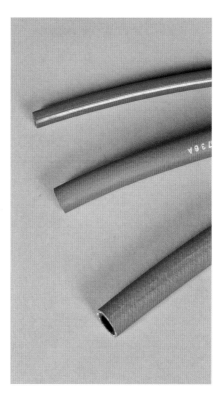

Air hose is available in ¼ in. ID, ⁵⁄₁₆ in. ID, and ⅜ in. ID. ¼ in. is not recommended for HVLP guns. Use only ⁵⁄₁₆ in. or ⅜ in.

Quick disconnect fittings are used with air hoses. They shut off the air when the hose is removed from the gun. They also allow you to use the same hose for operating other air tools like nail guns or staplers.

A regulator and a filter are used near the spray area for this stationary compressor setup.

What to look for in a compressor

When choosing a compressor, the most important criteria is the cfm it produces at a specific psi. It should be written on a plate or in the manual. If two figures are given, use the one that's rated at 40 psi. Don't worry about horsepower. Also important will be the air demands of the spray gun you intend to operate. You'll also have a choice between oilless and oil lubricated. Oil lubricated is generally more expensive, but runs quieter and cooler. Oilless is less expensive but a bit noisier and runs hotter. A big benefit of oilless is that it won't contaminate your air with oil.

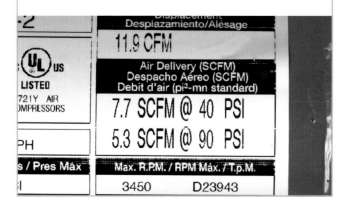

in humid weather) and possibly contaminants. These can collect in the storage tank, so filters are a good idea when operating a spray gun. Filters work best when they're as close to the spray gun as possible. You can purchase in-line filters which attach directly to the spray gun, or you can use a wall-mount filter that's mounted on a wall close to where you spray.

Spray guns

Spray guns come in two basic designs: siphon (also called suction) cups, and gravity cups. Siphon cups have the storage cup under the spray gun, while gravity guns have the cup on top.

Siphon cups

In a standard siphon cup, the finish is pushed upwards into the gun through a metal tube. A suction action created by air exiting the front of the gun moves the finish through the tube. When HVLP gained widespread use, it was found that the lower pressure from turbines wasn't enough to pull thicker finishes up into the gun. In response, manufacturers created a pressurized siphon cup (usually called a pressure cup). The cup is pressurized by an external or internal tube that diverts a small amount of air from the gun. This pushes the finish up into the gun.

Most turbine systems use pressurized siphon cups. In a compressor-driven system you have a choice between a pressurized or non-pressurized cup. Non-pressurized cups work fine for thinner to medium-viscosity finishes like stains and clear coats. If you plan on spraying thicker finishes like paint, always get a pressurized cup.

Gravity cups

With the cup mounted on top of the gun, gravity and atmospheric pressure push the finish down into the guns. Gravity guns aren't as fast as pressurized cup guns, but will handle thicker finishes like paint as long as you have the correct nozzle setup (see pp. 35–36). Gravity guns range from full size (about 20 oz. to 25 oz.) to smaller detail guns (about 4 oz. to 5 oz.) used for touch up and small project finishing. The small gravity guns sold as touch-up or detail guns use a low amount of air (4 cfm) and can typically be run on a small portable compressor.

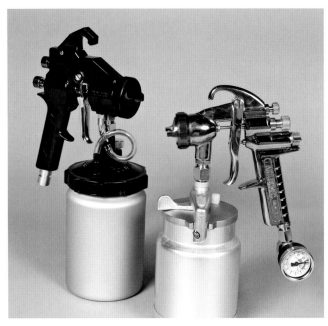

Siphon cups can run off a turbine (left) or a compressor. The turbine guns are always pressurized, while the compressor-driven versions can be pressurized or suction feed like the one shown.

Suction-feed guns are available in full-size versions like the gun on the right and inexpensive detail guns like the one on the left.

Gravity guns have the cup mounted on the top. They come in full-size guns as well as small detail guns like this one holding about 4 oz. of finish.

Turbine systems include everything you need when you buy them. Just add finish.

CFM vs. SCFM

Cubic feet per minute (CFM) is the measure of how much cubic feet of air moves per minute. This measurement may fluctuate depending on temperature, air pressure (the elevation at which you're using the compressor), and humidity. Standard cubic feet per minute (SCFM) was introduced as a measurement adjusted to standard temperature, pressure, and humidity. SCFM will appear on newer spray guns and compressors, but you might still see CFM. While an engineer may need very accurate and standardized flow rates, the two terms are interchangeable for consumers shopping for spray guns and compressors.

Choosing the right system

If you already own a compressor in good working condition, consider an HVLP conversion gun. If the compressor produces 7-8 cfm or more at 40 psi, you should be able to find a full-size siphon or gravity gun. If you have a pancake or similar small compressor that only produces 4 cfm or so at 40 psi, you can operate a gravity detail gun, but you'll be limited to stains, clear finishes, or highly thinned paints. Determine the cfm your compressor generates and purchase a gun that's equal to or less than this cfm figure. If it's a little higher (by 1 cfm) that's okay.

If you don't have a compressor, or it's not big enough, you're a candidate for a turbine system. There are advantages to turbines. They are more portable and everything you need will be included with the system. And there's a much shorter learning curve to set up and start using a turbine system. Since these systems are primarily marketed to DIYers, they have better instruction manuals.

On the plus side, compressor-driven conversion guns will give you more for your money. The very top of the line conversion guns are half the price of many entry-level turbine units. There are some very inexpensive turbine systems but these won't produce superior finishes. With a compressor-driven gun, you also have more control over the air to solve problems.

My recommendations

If you want the shortest learning curve and you're not sure about your compressor, or don't have one, look at a three-stage turbine for the most versatility in spraying

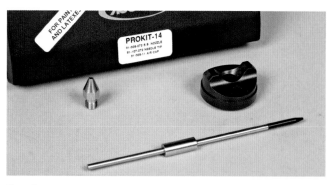

One size nozzle setup will not work for all finishes. Almost all guns come with a medium-viscosity nozzle. For thick coatings like paint, you'll need an extra setup.

Compressed air vs. turbine

	ADVANTAGES	DISADVANTAGES
Compressed Air HVLP	Less expensive if you already own a compressor	Needs filtration, correct hoses, fittings
	Less noisy	Heavier, not as portable
	Wider selection of spray gun types: suction, pressure cup, or gravity	A steeper learning curve, user needs to determine correct air pressure to operate gun
Turbine HVLP	Quicker learning curve	More expensive
	Sold as a complete package	Some models quite noisy
	No filtration	Large, bulky hose from turbine to gun
	Portable	Warm/hot air produced by turbine may cause problems with some finishes

A gravity stand supports a gravity gun while you're filling it.

stains and clear finishes. If you plan to spray paint, make sure you get an extra nozzle for thicker finishes if one is not included with the system.

If you have a good working compressor and want to do a variety of finishing on different sized projects with different finishes, consider a siphon-feed pressure-cup gun. (An extra nozzle setup may be required for thicker finishes and paint.) You can save money if you get a gravity HVLP gun; many of these are available for $100.00 or less. If you're mostly spraying small projects like guitars, bowls, or small tables, you can run an HVLP detail gravity gun even with a small compressor.

Accessories

Whichever system you buy, you need a few accessories, some of which you can make. One essential is a cleaning kit, which contains small sized brushes and wires to clean the small holes of your spray gun. Most are less than $30.00 and worth every penny.

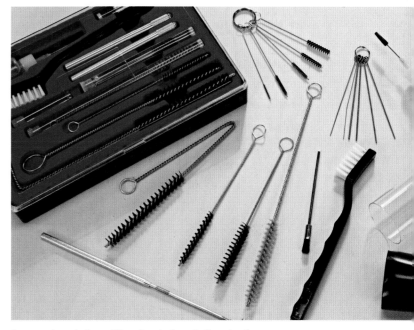

An assortment of small brushes help get all parts of a spray gun clean. It's essential that no finish remain to clog lines, tubes, and openings.

Riser blocks help you get a good finish right down to the base.

A nail board supports the work on the points of the screws. To make one, drive screws into a piece of plywood at regular distances.

If you own a gravity gun, you'll need a gravity stand for holding the gun upright as you fill it or when you're not using it. Many come with swing-away holders for strainers.

Supporting the work

You need a platform on which to finish. Sawhorses or a low table work in a pinch, but I like to be able to spin the work while spraying so I move around less. My favorite is a homemade low cart. It has platforms of two different heights for different types of projects. The tables spin easily without bearings or casters. An alternative is to get some Lazy Susan bearings which you can sandwich between two boards and place on sawhorses.

Nail boards allow you to finish both sides at the same time, which is efficient for things like tops and doors. Using ¼ in. plywood, drill drywall screws at intervals in the board which will support the work as you spray a finished side without marring it. You can make different sizes depending on the projects.

Riser blocks are square rectangles made from scrap wood, plywood, or MDF. The most valuable size is a 12-in. by 7-in. rectangle made from 3-in. wide pieces. They hold parts and case pieces off the spray table so you can spray the bottoms.

Building your own spray platform

You can easily build a spray platform. Everything you'll need should be available from your local home improvement center except the pipe floor flanges, which you can get from a plumbing supply store.

Construct the base with ¾-in. plywood according to the dimensions below. At one end secure the two fixed casters and at the other end secure the swivel casters. Using two fixed casters makes the platform easier to "steer."

In the center of the platform, secure the 2-in. floor flange. Attach the 18-in. piece of 2-in. black pipe to the flange. For the main table, use whatever size of

Materials list

(2) 4-in. fixed neoprene casters and 2–4-in. swivel neoprene casters
(1) 2-in. × 18-in. black pipe and 2-in. floor flange
(2) 1¼-in. black pipe floor flanges (if you want two tables of different heights, otherwise buy one flange)
(1) 1¼-in. × 28-in. black pipe
(1) 1¼-in. × 12-in. black pipe (if you want an extra table that's a shorter height)
(1) 1¾-in. washer
(2) 3½-in. (h) × 34½-in. (w) ¾-in. plywood or MDF
(2) 3½-in. (h) × 24-in. ¾-in. plywood or MDF
(1) 36-in. × 24-in. ¾-in. plywood or MDF
(1) 24-in. × 24-in. ¾-in. plywood for table
(1) 30-in. × 30-in. ¾-in. plywood (if you want two tables)
(2) 50-lb-bags of sand (optional)

A spray platform

TURNTABLE DETAILS

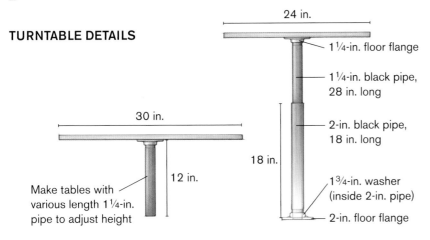

24 in.

1¼-in. floor flange

1¼-in. black pipe, 28 in. long

2-in. black pipe, 18 in. long

18 in.

1¾-in. washer (inside 2-in. pipe)

2-in. floor flange

30 in.

12 in.

Make tables with various length 1¼-in. pipe to adjust height

BASE DETAILS

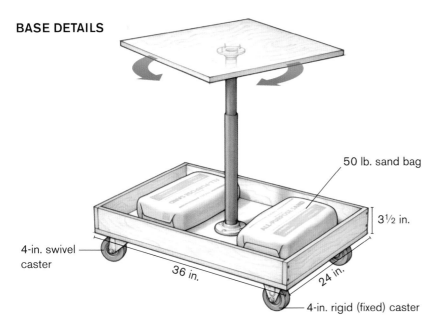

50 lb. sand bag

4-in. swivel caster

3½ in.

36 in.

24 in.

4-in. rigid (fixed) caster

¾-in plywood that's convenient for you. I suggest 24 in. by 24 in. Mark the center and install the 1¼-in. floor flange and then install the 18-in. piece of 1¼-in. pipe. This makes a waist-high table that accommodates most spray situations; however, I find a shorter table useful as well.

Make this second table using the 12-in. piece of 1¼ in. pipe. I find a larger top necessary for the shorter table, about 30 in. If you make a very large or heavy top, the platform may get a bit tippy. You can stabilize it by placing two 50-lb. bags of sand in the base.

You'll have the most versatility from the spray turntable if you make different height platforms. The high table should be about waist high so you can change the length of the pipe if necessary to customize.

It's easier to turn the work than to move around the piece you're spraying.

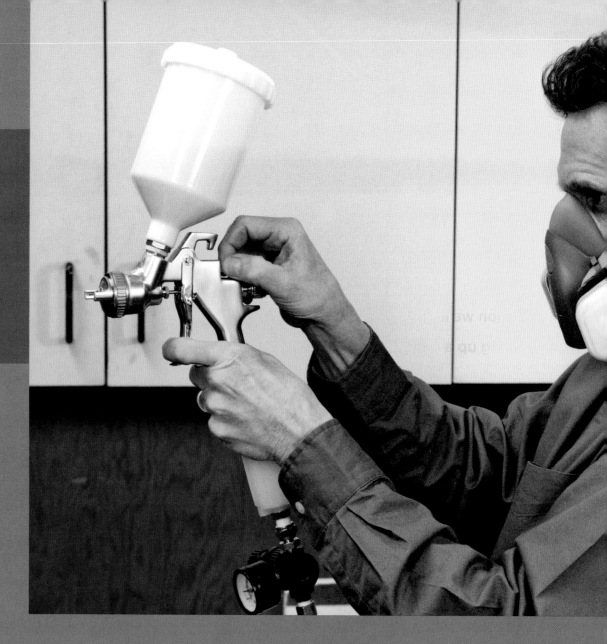

Setup

T
he source of air, whether a compressor or a turbine, is the heart of your spray system. It needs to be located and set up properly for good clean airflow. In this section we'll get into more detail about setting up a compressor- or turbine-driven HVLP system, then move right into the basics of good spray techniques.

Setting up a compressor system

Setting up a compressor-driven HVLP system requires more work than a turbine system. For a compressor-driven system, you'll need the following:

- a compressor whose cfm output matches or exceeds your spray gun's cfm usage at a comparable psi rating

- a filter to remove water and other contaminants

- an air hose to connect from your compressor to the gun

- quick disconnect fittings

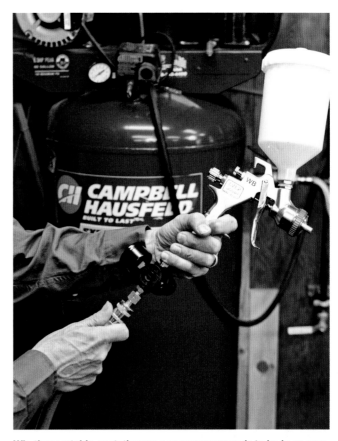

Whether portable or stationary, a compressor needs to be in an area where it can pull in clean, dry air, but far enough away from where you're spraying so that it doesn't recycle the overspray.

Compressor placement

A compressor can be either portable or stationary. You can keep a portable compressor near the area where you spray. However, you want to keep it far enough away so it doesn't pull in finish overspray through the air intake.

A basic compressor-driven HVLP system consists of a compressor, an air hose, a spray gun, and a filter. This in-line filter connects directly to the spray gun.

This stationary compressor feeds into ¾ in. black pipe that runs over to the spray area. The pipe is slanted toward the compressor so water condensing in the pipe flows back into the storage tank where it can be drained.

No matter which type of filter you use, it should be used as close to the spray gun as possible for it to be effective.

Make sure to place the compressor where it has clean air. Keep the distance about 15 ft. to 25 ft. from where you spray. If you have a stationary compressor that's further than 25 ft. from where you spray, you should consider running a ⅜-in. air hose or ½ in. ID to ¾ in. ID metal pipe to the spray area. Use black pipe or schedule L copper pipe. Slant the pipe towards the compressor.

Filter placement

In addition to air, a compressor will produce water droplets and vapor, as well as contaminants like small dirt particles and oil (if you have an oil-lubricated compressor). Depending on whether it's portable or stationary, you have several filter placement options.

Short runs If you run an air hose to the gun and the length of hose is 25 ft. or less, the simplest solution is to install an in-line water filter at the spray gun air inlet. These filters are available as disposable or re-usable. They trap water and most other contaminants. For occasional spraying, they are an inexpensive solution.

Long runs If you have a longer run of hose or are using hard pipe, you should install a wall-mounted water filter/regulator at the end of the pipe, close to the spray area. The regulator allows you to set the correct air to run your spray gun. If you have an older oil-lubricated compressor and you do more than occasional spraying, you may want to consider an all-in-one water/oil/dirt filter or separate water filters followed by oil and dirt filters. (Oil filters are also called coalescing filters.)

Air hose

The flexible air hose from your compressor, or the final filter if you hard pipe the compressor, is sold in several inside diameters: ¼ in., ⁵⁄₁₆ in., and ³⁄₈ in. For HVLP, avoid ¼ in. unless the length is shorter than 15 ft. Use ⁵⁄₁₆ in. for 15 ft. to 25 ft. runs, and ³⁄₈ in. for runs up to 50 ft. I don't recommend running more than 50 ft. of hose.

The most common types of hose material are rubber, PVC, or polyurethane. PVC and polyurethane are lighter than rubber. Most come with ¼ in. NPT (national pipe thread) male fittings on either end.

Quick disconnects

Portable compressors usually have a quick disconnect coupler fitting installed just after the output regulator. When you get a spray gun, you'll need to purchase three more fittings so it will work with the hose.

Quick disconnect fittings are divided into couplers and plugs. Couplers have a retractable sleeve and are the fittings that shut off the air when disconnected from a plug. Both are sold in female and male versions so make sure you get the correct ones for the hose. For the most common system you'll need two female plugs and one female coupler. To prevent leaks, use Teflon® plumber's tape to wrap the male fittings of the hose and gun before installing the couplers or plugs.

workSmart

Don't use ¼ in. ID hose over 15 ft., air reels, or re-coil hose with your HVLP compressor. All of these create a pressure drop internally and can cause atomization problems.

At most stores you have the choice of rubber air hose (left) or vinyl (right). The vinyl is usually lighter weight and more flexible.

"Quick-disconnect" systems are divided into male and female couplers (left) and plugs (right). They may not be inter-changeable between manufacturers so it's best to buy them in sets (coupler & plug).

To use a quick disconnect, push the plug into the coupler. To remove it, pull back the retractable collar or sleeve on the coupler, which pops the plug out. The air shut-off valve is contained within the coupler.

A wall-mounted water filter/regulator at the end of the pipe is best for long runs.

HVLP compressor-driven spray guns indicate the maximum inlet pressure near the air inlet. Running the gun at this pressure produces 10 psi air cap pressure (the maximum pressure allowed for HVLP) at the point where the finish comes out the front.

Setting the air pressure

Spray gun manuals typically do not tell you the exact air pressure to run your spray gun. The manual might list a maximum pressure, or maybe a range. If you have an HVLP gun, the manufacturer will list a "maximum" air pressure usually stamped on the handle near the air inlet. This pressure at the air inlet produces 10 psi tip pressure at the air cap. This is a good place to start. If you can't find an air pressure value stamped on the handle, look in the instruction manual.

Recommended PSI increase	
For 5/16-in. air hoses up to 15 ft.	Add 2 psi
For 5/16-in. air hoses up to 25 ft.	Add 3 psi
For 5/16-in. air hoses up to 50 ft.	Add 4 psi
For 3/8-in. air hoses up to 15 ft.	Add 1 psi
For 3/8-in. air hoses up to 25 ft.	Add 2 psi
For 3/8-in. air hoses up to 50 ft.	Add 3 psi

If you have a regulator installed at the gun, pull the trigger far enough to get air through the gun and look at the regulator gauge on the gun. Typically you turn the knob clockwise to increase the pressure and counterclockwise to decrease it. If you cannot get a high enough reading, then turn up the output regulator from your compressor. (Note that when you release the trigger, the gauge goes up to a higher reading, which is normal.)

If you don't have a regulator installed at the gun, you should set the output regulator that's on the compressor to the correct pressure described above. The only difference is that you have to compensate for pressure drop if you have more than 15 ft. of hose from the compressor to the gun. Use the chart at the bottom left to adjust the regulator a little higher to compensate.

The pressure that you just set is the highest pressure necessary to run your gun. Under most circumstances you can set it lower so you get less overspray. When you practice these steps later, you can make adjustments.

Setting up a turbine system

Compared to a compressor HVLP system, a turbine is much easier to set up. You don't have to worry about hoses and fittings. The turbine always produces warm and dry air, so there's no need for water filters. Since the turbine air operates at a maximum HVLP range, you don't have to worry about setting the air flow unless you want to turn it down. Simply plug the turbine in and place it where it will pull in dry and fresh air. (You don't want it to pull in overspray from the gun.)

Turbines usually come with 20-ft. to 30-ft. hoses. Connect the female swivel end to the turbine air output. Remove the cup from the gun and make sure the fluid pickup tube is bending away from you, toward the front of the gun. If not, loosen the hex nut that holds the cup top assembly to the gun and reposition it. Pour your strained finish into the cup and attach the cup to the gun. Then slip the coupler at the other end of the hose onto the air inlet of the gun.

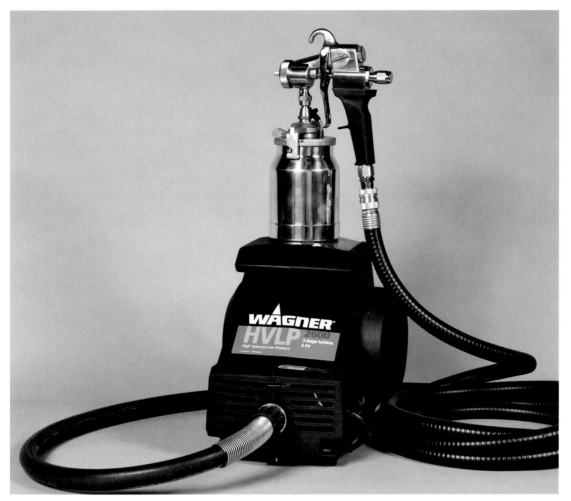

Turbines are sold as a complete packaged system consisting of a turbine, a HVLP spray gun, and an air hose. They are favored for the ease of use for first time sprayers and portability.

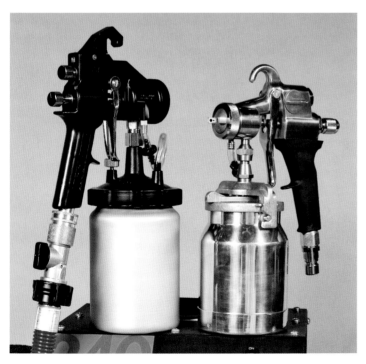

Turbine guns don't need air filters and operate at maximum HVLP range, so you don't need to regulate air flow unless you want to reduce it. Both these guns have air-flow regulators.

Air pressure setup with a compressor

1

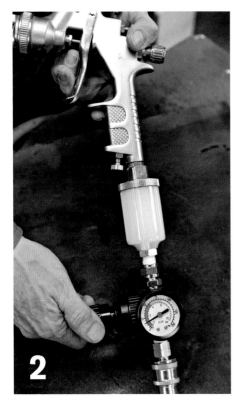

2

3

One of the main differences between a turbine-driven HVLP system and a compressor-driven system is that you have complete control over the air pressure that runs the gun. Getting this set precisely keeps the amount of overspray down while producing the best finish possible. The most common situation in a small shop is a portable compressor. In this example, we're assuming you have 50 ft. or less of ⅜-in. hose from your compressor to the gun and a mini-regulator at the gun. Note that the pressure settings are different without a mini-regulator.

1. **Install the inline filter at the gun.** Wrap Teflon plumber's tape around the threads of the gun air intake valve to prevent air leaks.

2. **Install the regulator** below the inline filter, if your spray gun has a regulator. It's okay to install the regulator first, then the filter.

3. **Set the output regulator of your compressor** to 20 psi above the maximum pressure of the spray gun. If you don't have a mini-regulator on your gun, set the pressure at 3 psi above the stated maximum for the spray gun.

4. **Adjust to the correct operating pressure** with the mini-regulator. Make sure the trigger is pulled to let air through.

workSmart

When setting the air pressure for your gun, always pull the trigger just enough to get air flowing through the gun. This will insure that you duplicate what the gun is using in air flow when spraying finish.

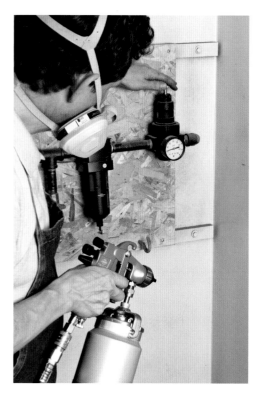

If you have a regulator/filter unit near the spray area, or don't use a mini-regulator at the gun, adjust the correct operating pressure for the spray gun with the wall mounted regulator (shown) or your compressor output regulator.

Basic turbine setup

No matter which turbine system you get, the basic setup is pretty straightforward. Other than making sure you have the right nozzle setup for the finish you're using, there's not a lot that can go wrong for first-time turbine spray users. However, there are a few things you need to get right so the system works correctly.

1. **Orient the fluid pickup tube** toward the front of the gun.

2. **Connect the external check valve** to the gun and the cup. (On most turbine guns, the external check valve is mounted between two pieces of clear tube.)

3. **Locate the air opening** on guns with a splash guard and orient it toward the back of the gun. The splash guard prevents finish from constantly clogging the check valve.

4. **Connect the female end** of the air hose to the turbine unit.

5. **Install the quick disconnect coupler** to the air inlet of the turbine gun.

workSmart

Two things that may cause problems with first-time turbine users are the air flow control and check valve. First, always spray with the air wide open if you have an air flow control valve on your spray gun or a turbine speed control. Second, make sure the check valve is allowing air to pressurize the cup. These can frequently clog, particularly if the gun tips over. If it does you'll have to clean out the valve or replace it.

Spray gun basics

efore pulling the trigger on a spray gun, you should spend some time familiarizing yourself with its operation. Fortunately most spray guns operate on a very simple and basic design so it's not too hard to get acquainted with how they work.

Getting to know your spray gun

All spray guns operate on the same general principles, but they may differ slightly depending on whether you have a turbine gun or a compressed air gun. In both cases, incoming air from a compressor or a turbine is directed into a finish stream exiting the front of the gun which turns the liquid finish into small droplets. This is called atomization. A spray gun has two main controls which adjust the fluid delivery valve and the fan width control.

Viscosity, nozzles, and thinning

Viscosity refers to the thickness of a finish. It's important because to spray any finish properly you have to match the nozzle/needle and air caps to the viscosity of the finish. While it's possible to describe finishing materials in a generic sort or way, like "water-thin," or "heavy cream-like," the best way to determine viscosity is to measure it with a viscosity cup. Some manufacturers supply one with the system, but most do not. The most common viscosity cup that's affordable is a Ford® #4, which can be used with all stains and clear finishes. It won't work with thick paints because the opening is too small. Viscosity is measured by timing how long it takes the finish to flow through the opening at the bottom of the cup. With this information, you can pick the correct nozzle to use in your spray gun.

Viscosity cups

Plastic Ford #4 cup

Iwata® NK-2 stainless steel industrial cup

Generic plastic cup provided by the manufacturer

workSmart

As a general rule, use a smaller size nozzle and needle (and air cap if sold as a set) for thinner finishes, and a larger size set for thicker finishes. To finesse things, you can use a smaller size nozzle set than normally used to slow down the rate of finish and a larger one to speed up the rate of finish delivery.

How a spray gun works

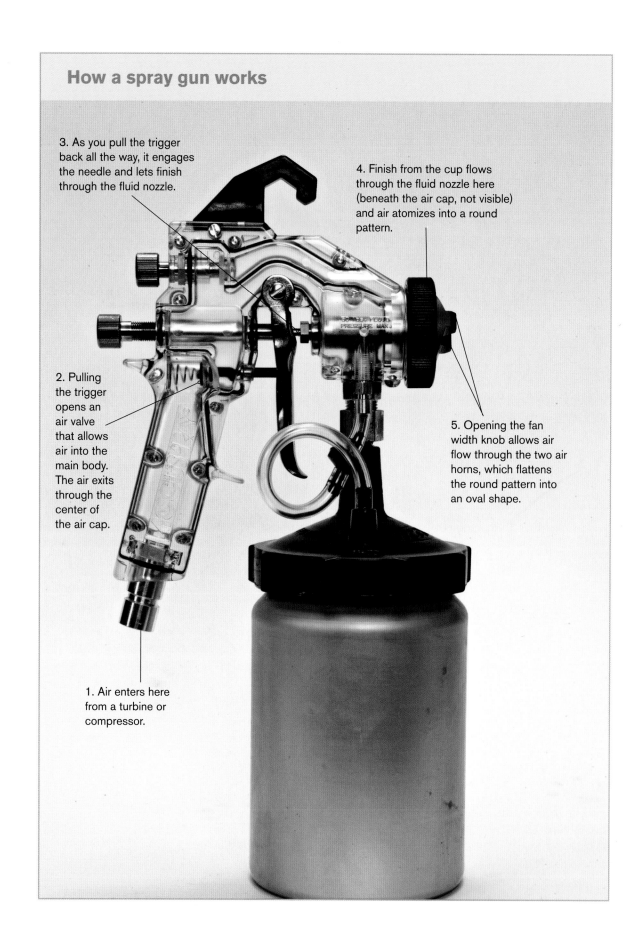

3. As you pull the trigger back all the way, it engages the needle and lets finish through the fluid nozzle.

4. Finish from the cup flows through the fluid nozzle here (beneath the air cap, not visible) and air atomizes into a round pattern.

2. Pulling the trigger opens an air valve that allows air into the main body. The air exits through the center of the air cap.

5. Opening the fan width knob allows air flow through the two air horns, which flattens the round pattern into an oval shape.

1. Air enters here from a turbine or compressor.

Nozzles, needles, and air caps

Spray gun manufacturers sell nozzles and matching needles sized in millimeters or inches. (The nozzle and needle are always matched to each other.) If the actual size isn't used, the manufacturer may assign the set a number like #2 or #4.

Once you've timed your finish and determined the viscosity, you can match it to the suggested nozzle set. Some manufacturers provide this information. If yours doesn't, you can also reference the chart (see p. 40) for the correct nozzle set.

With some manufacturers, the air cap may be replaced. In that case, you may purchase a nozzle, needle, and air cap as a matched set. If you only plan to spray

The needle is one of the most delicate parts of the spray gun. The precisely machined end must seat perfectly within the nozzle or the gun will leak.

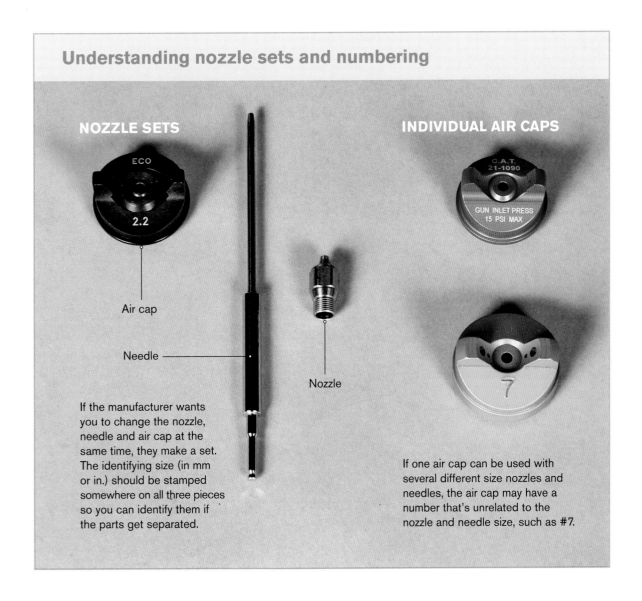

Understanding nozzle sets and numbering

NOZZLE SETS

ECO

2.2

Air cap

Needle

Nozzle

If the manufacturer wants you to change the nozzle, needle and air cap at the same time, they make a set. The identifying size (in mm or in.) should be stamped somewhere on all three pieces so you can identify them if the parts get separated.

INDIVIDUAL AIR CAPS

C.A.T. 21-1090

GUN INLET PRESS 15 PSI MAX

7

If one air cap can be used with several different size nozzles and needles, the air cap may have a number that's unrelated to the nozzle and needle size, such as #7.

one finish viscosity, you can use one setup. On the other hand, if you want to spray stains, clear finishes, and thick paints, you might need as many as three separate setups.

Always install the fluid nozzle first. If you don't, you may damage the more delicate needle. If you must install the nozzle with the needle in the gun, retract the needle by pulling back completely on the trigger first.

Thinning

Thinning is discouraged by most manufacturers. When you add thinner to solvent-based finishes you increase the amount of volatile organic compounds (VOCs) entering the air. With waterborne finishes, adding too much water will alter the chemistry of the finish, and you'll have flow-out or performance problems.

That said, thinning can be a useful problem-solving technique. Or you may need to thin a thick finish to match a smaller nozzle set if you don't have a larger one on hand. Generally, you can't go wrong as long as you don't thin too much. Waterborne finishes can typically tolerate a maximum 10 percent thinning with water, while solvent based finishes tolerate far more thinning, as high as 100 percent (one part thinner to one part finish). You must always add water to a latex-type paint to spray it.

If you have a finish whose viscosity measures too high for the nozzle set you have, try spraying it first. If it's

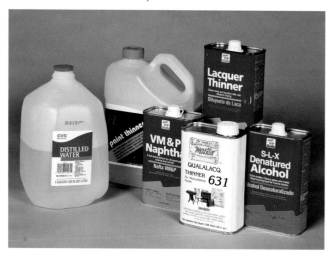

From left to right: Use distilled water for thinning waterborne finishes. Paint thinner can be used for cleanup of oil-based finishes, but use naphtha when thinning oil-based products for spraying. Generic lacquer thinner can be used for cleanup, but follow the manufacturer's suggested thinner for lacquer. Denatured alcohol is for thinning shellac.

Thinning is a lot easier if you use graduated paint mixing cups available from home centers and paint stores.

close to the range for the nozzle you have, it may spray well enough. If it doesn't, try adding thinner in 5 percent increments until it sprays without sputtering.

Viscosity and nozzle relationship

The extreme scenario is a nozzle that is too small for the finish you want to spray. The finish either won't come through at all (the gun won't spray), or the finish dribbles out of the nozzle and the gun sputters. On the other hand, if the nozzle set is too large, the finish won't atomize well and you get a textured surface called orange peel (see p. 111). Ideally, the finish should exit the fluid nozzle in a continuous stream without breaking.

In some instances you can use a slightly smaller or larger nozzle. If you use a nozzle set that's slightly smaller by one or two steps, you can restrict the rate at which the finish comes out. This makes it easier to do more controlled and precise spraying for small items or detail

warning

You may see "Do Not Thin" on the can of your finish. Adding thinner to the finish increases the VOCs and may put it over the legal limit. You may not be arrested for thinning your finish, but always try spraying the finish without thinning.

work or for touch up. A slightly larger nozzle set will allow the finish to come out at a faster rate beneficial for exterior painting or staining, where speed is desired.

Adjusting the spray pattern

Controlling the finish and the way it's atomized is important when you spray the different parts of your project. You may want a big, wide pattern delivered at a high rate for large tops like tables, or you may want a controlled, more precise pattern for edges, legs, and slats. Adjusting the proper spray pattern is essential to keep overspray to a minimum and improves the quality of your spraying.

Essential accessories

Always strain the finish before spraying to eliminate impurities that can clog the gun. Choose a filter appropriate to the style of gun you have.

Finishes flow out best at a specific thickness. Many manufacturers specify this thickness as "wet-mil" thickness. You measure this thickness with an inexpensive device known as a wet-mil gauge. It's a piece of stamped metal that has notches cut into the edges on all four sides. You can get one at good paint stores and from on-line spray suppliers. Use the side numbered from 1 to 6.

Ideally, the finish should exit through the nozzle in a straight line. You can test this out with a gravity gun by disconnecting the air and pulling the trigger with finish in the cup.

A wet-mil gauge. Use the side numbered 1 to 6.

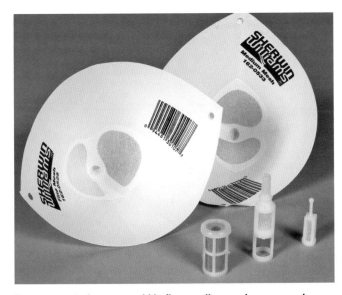

Paper cone strainers are sold in fine, medium, and coarse grades. The fine and medium ones shown here work with all paints, stains and clear finishes. The in-gun strainers shown in front are installed somewhere in the spray gun. Ideally you should use both.

workSmart

You can certainly get to know the controls on your spray gun by practicing with finish, but it's easier to use solvent. I recommend practicing with denatured alcohol. It will flush out any residue from manufacturing the gun (like machining oil) and shouldn't interfere with any of the finishes used in this book if a small amount is left in the gun.

Changing a nozzle set

You'll have to change the nozzle set if you spray a different viscosity finish. If the needle is hard to pull backward, you can grasp it with some pliers. When putting the needle back in, I like to roll the shaft right behind the tip with a little gun lube.

1. **Remove the air cap retaining ring** and take off the air cap (sometimes they are attached together).

2. **Remove the fluid control knob** and needle compression spring.

3. **Pull the needle** out backward.

4. **Remove the fluid nozzle** with a wrench or the manufacturer's supplied wrench.

5. **Replace the nozzle, then the needle.** Then replace the compression spring and fluid control knob.

6. **Orient the air cap** to the correct position by loosening the retaining ring to position it correctly.

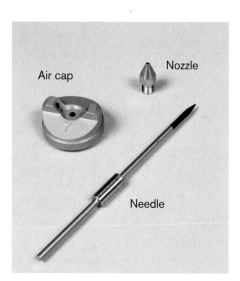

Air cap

Nozzle

Needle

When you change sizes on a spray gun, you will typically change three parts: the air cap, the nozzle, and the needle.

1

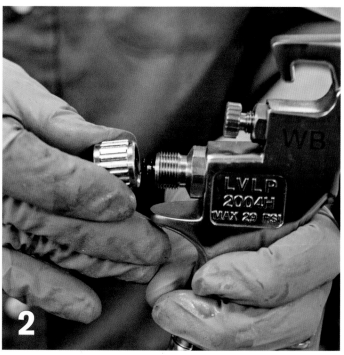

2

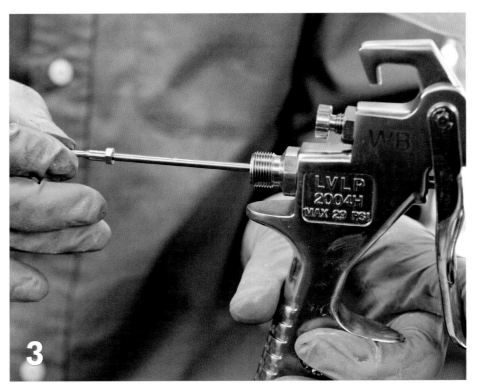

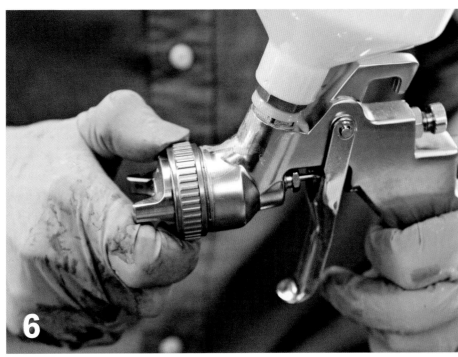

Measuring viscosity

You'll need a watch with a second hand and the viscosity cup to time the finish. Make sure the cup is clean and there is no residual dried finish in the hole at the bottom. If there is, soak it in some lacquer thinner and clean the hole with a small brush.

1. **Pour the finish** (at room temperature) into a plastic mixing cup.

2. **Dunk the viscosity cup** into the plastic mixing cup until the rim of the cup is slightly covered with finish.

3. **Note the time** as you pull the cup out. Hold the cup approximately 6 in. above the container.

4. **Continue to monitor the time,** watching the finish flow. The finish will gradually drain.

5. **Note the time that the finish stops** or breaks (is no longer contiguous).

Generic viscosity

	Viscosity time in seconds with Ford #4	Gravity (mm)	Suction cup (siphon feed/ non-pressurized) (mm)	Suction cup (pressure feed) (mm)
Water thin	12–16	1.1	1.3–1.4	0.7
	17–25	1.2–1.3	1.5	.8–1.0
	25–35	1.5	1.7	1.1
Medium	35–40	1.5–1.7	1.9	1.1–1.2
	40–45	1.7	2.2	1.2–1.3
	45–55	1.9		1.3–1.5
Thick	55+	2.2	N/R	1.5–1.7
				1.7–2.2

workSmart

When measuring viscosity make sure the finish is at room temperature or between 65°F to 75°F degrees. When the finish is too cold, it will be thicker and give you a false reading. Plus, cold finishes don't spray well. You can bring the finish inside overnight if you work in a cold environment. To avoid cold finish, don't store it on a concrete floor in the winter.

Adjusting the fluid and fan controls

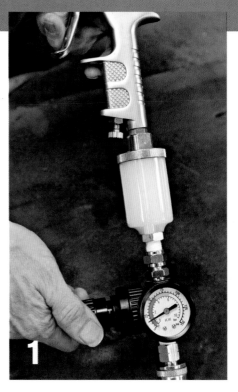

workSmart

Some turbine guns do not have a variable control valve; instead, the fan width and shape is changed by turning the air cap.

To get a feel for the two main controls on your gun, you can practice with some denatured alcohol solvent. The fluid valve determines how fast the finish comes out, while the fan width adjustment changes the atomized finish shape from small and round to wide and oval shaped.

1. **Pour some denatured alcohol in the cup.** Turn both the fluid delivery and fan width valves completely clockwise to close them. Set your compressor to the pressure necessary to run the gun if using a compressed air gun.

2. **Pull the trigger completely backward** and turn the fluid valve counter-clockwise until a round pattern of finish is visible. Typically this is two to three full turns. Continue opening the valve and note how the amount of atomized solvent increases. Turning it clockwise decreases the output until it shuts off.

3. **Locate the fan width control** and turn it counter-clockwise. As the fan width opens up, you may notice the finish volume decrease.

4. **To increase the spray pattern,** you may have to go back to the fluid control and open it up until you see a nice wide pattern of finish.

5. **Rotating the air cap** on any gun 90 degrees will switch the orientation of the spray from vertical to horizontal.

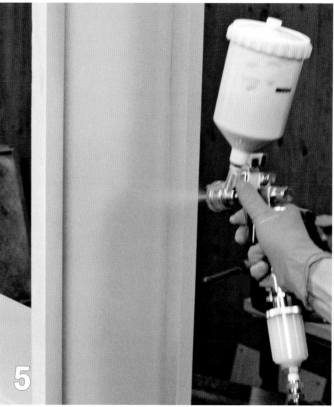

Straining finish

A gravity gun holder/strainer.

You should always strain the finish that goes into your spray gun. This will remove impurities like dirt and clumps that will clog the nozzle when you spray or come out on your sprayed surface. There are several ways to do this depending on the type of gun you have.

If you have a gravity gun, purchase a gravity gun holder/strainer. This allows you to strain the finish with a paper cone type strainer as you fill the cup. It's also a holder that keeps the gun upright when it is filled with finish.

If you have a bottom-feed gun, you can hold the paper strainer as you fill the cup. Or you can use a gun strainer. It attaches to the fluid pickup tube on bottom-cup guns. (For gravity guns, there are strainers that fit either inside the cup or inside the gun opening where the cup attaches.) It's fine to use the gun strainers with stains and clear finishes. With thicker finishes and paints, gun strainers tend to clog quickly and can really slow the fluid output down, or stop it completely.

A gun strainer for a bottom-cup gun.

A gun strainer for a gravity gun.

Using a wet mil gauge

A wet mil gauge will tell you how much finish you're putting down expressed in mils—or 1/1,000th of an inch. Putting down the proper thickness of finish insures that it will flow out correctly. A big problem for first-time sprayers is either putting down a finish too thin (the finish can't level out to a smooth finish) or too thick (the finish will run or entrap air bubbles). With most consumer finishes, you'll aim for a minimum of 2 mil and a maximum of 4 mil.

1. **Spray some finish** onto a practice piece or cardboard.

2. **Put the wet mil gauge firmly down** (using the side that's numbered 1 to 6) on the surface.

3. **Drag the mil gauge** about 2 in. to 3 in. and examine the troughs left beginning with number 1. The first notch that doesn't make a trough is your wet mil thickness.

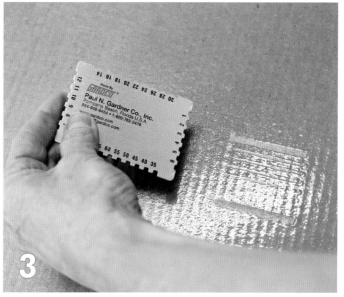

Basic spray techniques

B efore you jump right into a project, it's a good idea to practice spraying on some cardboard. This will get you used to working with your gun and setup, the area where you will be spraying, and the finishing product you're using.

Always spray toward the exhaust fan. Start at the edge closest to you and move the gun in successive passes toward the fan.

Strategies for spraying different types of surfaces

A large flat surface is the best surface to start spraying. You won't get into trouble with runs and drips and, if you make some rookie mistakes like being a little heavy handed with the finish, it will still flow out and level well.

The hardest thing to overcome with spraying a horizontal surface is the fear of tipping the gun too far forward. Ideally, the gun should spray parallel with the surface at about a 6 in. distance. Orient your piece so it's at a comfortable height (about waist-high). Before you pull the trigger, move the gun to the far end of the piece, holding the air hose with your free hand. By checking in advance, you know that you will be able to reach the far end comfortably.

Lock your wrist and forearm and move the gun in a straight line. Don't arc the gun. The gun should always be parallel to the surface, about 5 in. to 6 in. away. Turbine-

Cardinal points for spraying a flat surface

Lock your forearm and wrist.

About 6 in.

Overlap each new pass at least 50% over the previous.

Width of pattern

47

Turn the air cap 90 degrees so the spray pattern is oriented horizontally. Test on a small piece of scrap.

driven guns are usually held closer than compressor-driven guns. Always overlap the previous pass by at least 50 percent.

Spraying vertical surfaces

Vertical surfaces are harder to spray because you must lay down a coat thick enough to dry smooth, but not so heavy that it drips. To get the best coverage, change the orientation of the fan by rotating the air cap. This also makes the gun easier to use because you don't have to tilt it sideways. Raise the piece off the floor with blocks so

you can get the edges and trigger the gun just like you're spraying a flat surface, overlapping each pass by at least 50 percent. Before you start, make sure you have the correct gun speed and have the gun positioned at the right distance from the workpiece.

Many finishers who experience difficulties getting a good smooth finish spray a quick "tack" coat, which is a light deposit of finish. To spray a tack coat, adjust the fluid delivery valve to spray less finish or move the gun faster. Wait a few minutes then go over the tack coat with a heavier coat.

Spraying interiors

I always spray the interior of a cabinet first because these surfaces are less visible. If possible, remove the back of the cabinet. If you spray with the back on, the overspray is trapped and can't escape, resulting in an inferior finish. If you're building the cabinet yourself, you can pre-finish the back before assembly. Spray toward the exhaust fan and raise the project off the spray table. Re-orient the air cap as necessary to avoid tilting the gun.

Spraying the inside of a cabinet is much easier if you follow a logical pattern. Start with the four inside corners, and spray the underside of the top, the two sides, and finally the bottom, in that order. Since the bottom and sides are typically the most critical areas of the inside, these should be the last areas sprayed.

If you make your own furniture, always design the back so it can be fastened after finishing. This makes spraying inside the cabinet a lot easier.

When you spray the inside of a cabinet, start in the corners and turn down the inlet pressure so that the finish can reach the corners and edges.

Spraying complicated projects

Spraying something complex like a chair, stool, or anything else that has a lot of surfaces requires more strategy than spraying flats. A turntable spray platform is a must with complex projects. Otherwise, you'll be constantly moving around with the spray gun, or worse, trying to move the project with wet finish on it.

Plan your spray strategy by going through a dry run with the spray gun and divide the session into two parts. In the first session, you'll work all the undersides and inside surfaces that don't get seen as much. Remember to leave an unfinished area so that you can turn the project and access the areas that still need to be finished. In the second session, you'll spray areas that are more visible. Surfaces that get the most wear and tear like a chair seat are now flat. You can apply a little heavier finish, and it won't drip. If you do a lot of complicated things and have to maneuver a spray gun into tight corners, use a small detail gun.

Spray the underside or inside first, as those areas are less visible.

A small detail gun will spray into smaller areas much easier than a full-size gun.

Spraying flat surfaces

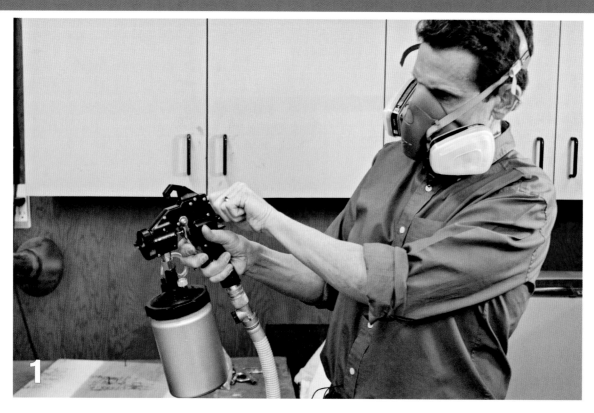

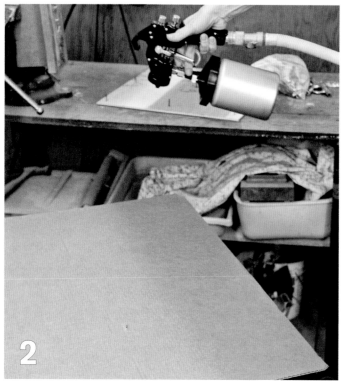

I f you're new to spraying, practice on a flat surface first using cardboard or scrap plywood. While flats seem the easiest to spray, you have to get the right sequence to avoid pattern streaks. Called "banding," pattern streaks show up as a striped effect.

1. **Set the gun** up for a 6 in. to 8 in. fan width and open up the fluid valve several turns.

2. **Pull the trigger completely** about 3 in. from the near edge. Move the gun until you see a wet coat of finish laying down, but not so slow that the finish "puddles." Release the trigger when you are 3 in. off the opposite edge.

3. **Overlapping the first coat** by 50 percent or more, lay down another coat, exactly as the first.

4. **Repeat the previous steps** until you reach the far edge. Remember to start spraying at the edge closest too you and work the pattern away from you. This "chases" the overspray off the far edge, where the fan exhaust will pull it away.

5. **Use a mil gauge** to check whether you're achieving the right thickness of finish.

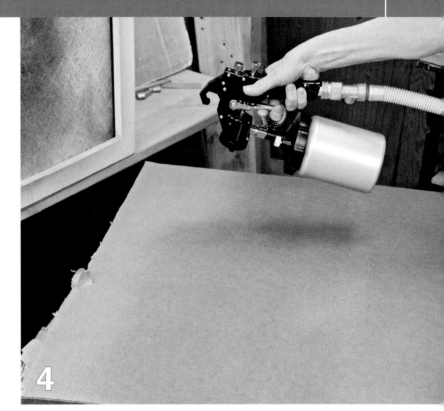

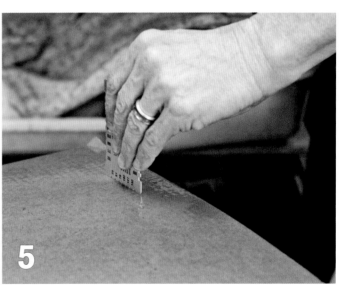

workSmart

It's much easier to spray the larger parts of a project without things like drawer pulls and knobs in the way. Remove knobs and pulls and spray them separately. You can hold them securely on a board with a drywall screw or double-sided tape so they don't blow around.

Spraying vertical surfaces

The main problems with verticals are drips and runs, so try not to thin the finish too much. Also, have good lighting so you avoid working in a shadow. You'll follow the same basic sequence as for spraying a flat surface.

1. **Orient the air cap** so it's spraying a horizontal (side to side) pattern. Starting at the bottom, trigger the gun to start the finish flow at about 3 in. from the closest edge.

2. **Continue on to the top** and off the edge.

3. **Overlap the prior coat by at least 50 percent** and continue on until you reach the other edge.

4. **Check for any missed areas** using backlighting. Respray if necessary.

workSmart

If you do get a drip, wipe it quickly with the tip of your finger and respray immediately.

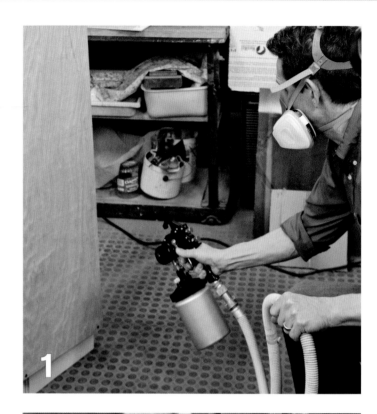

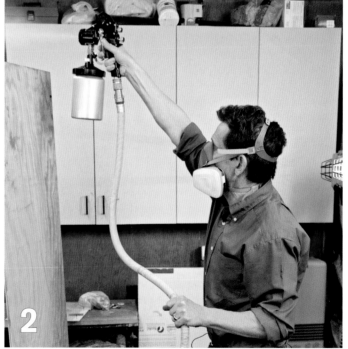

Spraying interiors

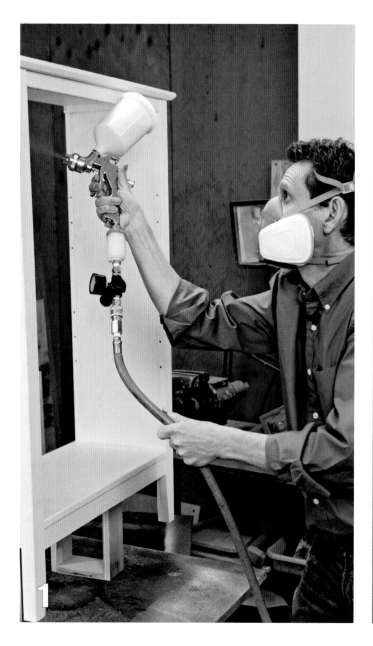

The more you can disassemble your project into separate parts to spray it the better. Try to spray toward the fan so it pulls the overspray away from surfaces you're not spraying. You may be able to reduce the amount of atomizing air to reduce overspray.

1. **Spray the inside four corners first,** starting at the top. Use a smaller diameter spray pattern.

2. **Open up the fan width** and spray the underside of the top.

3. **Spray the two vertical sides;** make sure you turn the air cap to change the fan pattern.

4. **Spray the bottom last.** You can apply a heavier coat here since it's flat. If you see a cloud of overspray inside the cabinet, you can pull the trigger just enough so air comes through and use it to blow the overspray towards the exhaust fan.

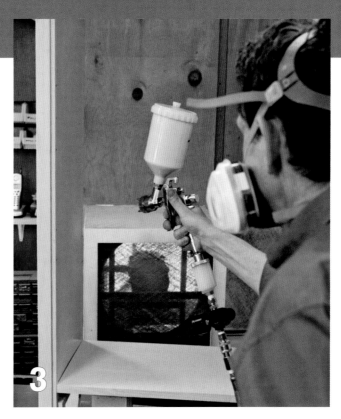

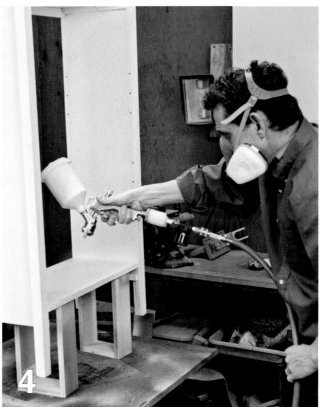

Spraying complicated projects

This chair is typical of a project with many complicated surfaces to spray. Generally, if you follow the "inside-first, outside-last" strategy, you should get good results. Whenever possible, spray a chair on a revolving platform so that you can access many sides without changing your position.

1. **Drive screws in the four leg bottoms** so the chair will be raised up from the platform.

2. **Turn the chair upside down.** Spray the underside of the seat and the other least visible parts. At this point, you can fine-tune the spray pattern so you get a wet enough finish but no drips or runs.

3. **Spray the underside** of the seat.

4. **Spray the back and underside** of the crest rail and arms (if the chair has them).

5. **Grasp the chair on an unfinished area** and flip it over on the spray platform. Spray the rest of the chair but leave the chair seat bottom for last.

6. **Now you can apply a heavier coat** on the seat because it's flat.

3

4

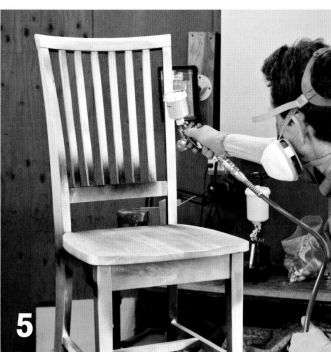

5

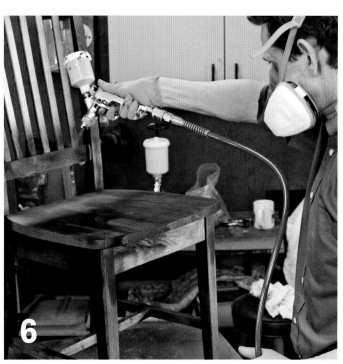

6

Spraying both sides with a nail board

1

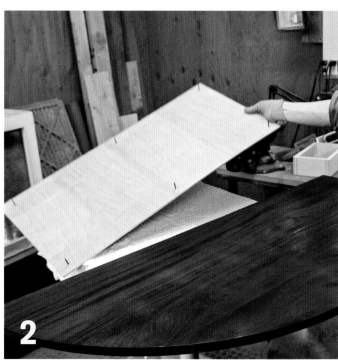

2

3

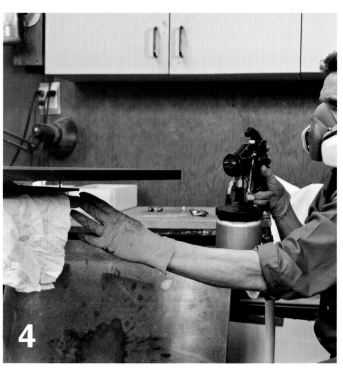

4

Spraying allows you to eliminate one of the biggest headaches associated with hand application of a finish to doors and other items that have two show sides: drip-overs. You'll need a nail board sized to the project. Always remember to avoid spraying the edges until you turn it over, otherwise you'll have nowhere to grab it.

1. **Place your top** or door with the best side down on some soft cloths or a towel. Spray a wet coat on the non-show side. Do not spray the edges yet.

2. **Holding it by the edges,** carefully remove the workpiece from the spray platform. Put down the nail board.

3. **Pick up the piece by the edges** and place it wet-side down on the nail board. Get a helper if it's a large piece.

4. **Spray the edges,** holding the gun parallel to the edge.

5. **Raise the gun** and spray the area where the edge meets the top at a 45-degree angle.

6. **Then spray** the show side.

┃workSmart

If you move the piece off the spray platform to dry, grab the nail board so you move it and the piece at the same time.

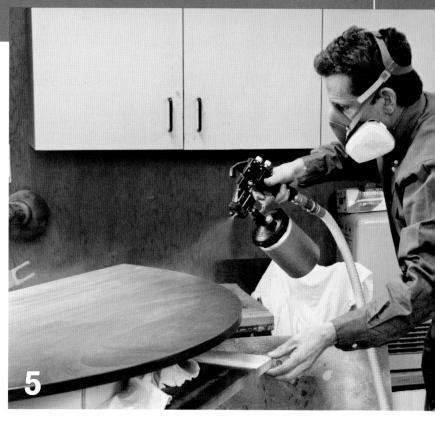

Spraying clear finishes

Clear finishes will probably be the first kind of finishes you'll spray. This class of finishes offers you the most choices, from lacquers and urethanes to varnishes and shellac. Most of these finishes are available as waterborne or solvent-borne, so you can choose one that suits your equipment and the area where you will spray.

Spraying allows you to take advantage of finishes that dry quickly, like lacquers and shellac. These finishes are difficult to apply by hand because they dry so fast. But when you spray, a fast-drying finish is better because it doesn't allow time for

These finishes are the most common ones you'll find at most home centers and hardware stores. Waterborne finishes (on the right) are replacing the solvent-based finishes on the left. In some states, solvent-based finishes may no longer be available.

airborne dust or debris to settle in it before it's dry. So don't grab a can of your favorite brushing polyurethane to spray. It dries too slowly. Instead, see if there's a faster-drying version of your favorite finish that's better suited to spraying. Once you get used to finishes that dry in minutes, you'll never go back to conventional finishes.

Types of clear finishes

Clear finishes are broadly grouped into waterborne (thins with water) and solvent-borne (thins with a solvent like lacquer thinner, alcohol, or mineral spirits). There are several classes of finish suitable for spraying.

Lacquer is the finish used on most factory furniture that doesn't require an extra durable finish. It's good for tables, chairs, bookcases, chests and bedroom furniture. Lacquer is available as both waterborne and solvent-borne. Solvent-borne lacquer may not be available in areas that have VOC restrictions, so don't be surprised if you can't find it.

Solvent-based lacquers are either consumer-grade finishes applied with a brush (third from left) or professional finishes applied by spraying. If you want to use the professional lacquers you'll have to find a commercial store in your area willing to sell it to you. Waterborne lacquers (on the right) are much easier to find.

The pre-mixed shellac on the left is either waxy or dewaxed. Always use the dewaxed grade when using as a sealer. The flakes on the right are also sold as dewaxed or waxy. They require dissolving in denatured alcohol to make a sealer or finish.

Nowadays, varnishes are seldom found in home centers, having largely been replaced by oil-base polyurethane (a type of varnish). Specialty woodworking or paint stores may carry them. Waterborne varnishes (far right) are available through mail order.

You may not think so, but waterborne polyurethanes dry to the touch much faster than oil-based polyurethanes. Oil-based polyurethanes have an amber color that looks good on most woods, while waterborne polyurethanes tend to be colorless.

Waterborne lacquers may be identified by the word acrylic in the name or list of ingredients. The most common solvent-borne lacquer is called nitrocellulose lacquer. While not as fast drying, brushing lacquer can be used if you cannot find spray lacquer.

Polyurethane is also available as waterborne or solvent-borne. It can be used when you need more durability for kitchen cabinets and situations where a harder wearing finish is required. Waterborne versions dry much quicker and don't have the distinctive amber color that the solvent-borne polyurethanes have. Some manufacturers make a "fast-dry" or "quick-dry" polyurethane that's better for spray application than brushing polyurethane.

Shellac is a solvent-borne finish primarily used as a sealer, but sometimes it's used as a finish for antique furniture. Shellac is a very quick-drying finish whose odor isn't particularly objectionable (alcohol is the solvent). There are two types, waxy and dewaxed. Unless the product specifically says it's dewaxed, it is a waxy grade. Shellac is sold either premixed or in flakes that are mixed with denatured alcohol to make a liquid finish. The amount of shellac expressed in pounds mixed into a gallon of denatured alcohol is called the "cut" or ratio of shellac to alcohol. The most common cut to use as a finish is a 2 lb. cut, but 1 lb. and ½ lb. cuts are used as sealers or as stain controllers called "wash-coats." Pre-mixed shellacs have instructions on the can for diluting to lighter cuts.

Varnish is primarily solvent-borne. Varnishes are becoming increasingly hard to find and have largely been replaced by polyurethane. Varnishes dry slowly and most people find the odor objectionable. Spar or marine varnishes are formulated for exterior use. There are a few waterborne varnishes available.

Sealers

Some clear finishes require a separate sealer, others are self-sealing. All waterborne finishes are generally self-sealing, as are solvent-borne polyurethanes. Solvent-borne lacquer should always be used with a lacquer sanding sealer, because it doesn't sand very well.

Sanding the sealer coat gives you a much smoother final finish. When you use a sealer, the most important thing to check is whether it's compatible with the top-coat. If you are unsure, shellac can be used as a universal sealer with any finish as long as it's dewaxed. You may consider using it when you need a very quick-drying sealer coat, or when you want to add a little amber color to a water-clear finish. It's also a good idea to use when you are re-finishing something, as it isolates any residue from stripping or other contamination that might cause

Always make sure the sealer you use is compatible with the final finish. Some sealers, like the solvent lacquer sealer on the far left, won't work with finishes other than solvent lacquer. The dewaxed shellac on the right is as close as you can get to a universal sealer.

drying or adhesion problems with the new finish. If you decide to spray it as the sealer and finish, you can use any of the grades available, either pre-mixed or shellac that you make yourself from flakes. The easiest cut to spray is a 2 lb. cut.

The bottom half of this sample board was sealed with a dewaxed shellac sealer first. It adds a warmer color under the clear waterborne finish applied over it. The top half shows what the wood looks like with the waterborne finish only.

Spraying lacquer sanding sealer

Spraying lacquer sanding sealer is a great way to learn to use your spray gun. Because the sealer is sanded after it dries, you can correct minor problems with flow-out or drips. I thin the sealer 1:1 with lacquer thinner.

1. **Thin the sanding sealer** with an equal amount of lacquer thinner in a mixing cup.

2. **Prop the piece up on the riser blocks.** Start spraying the inside first. This will allow you to make any last minute adjustments. Set up the gun for this part of the project with the proper fan width (in this case 4 in.) and medium flow rate. Spray the inside.

3. **For table legs, start with the inside** and then move to the outside of the legs.

4. **Then spray the sides** (here, the aprons).

5. **Spray the top last** (see p. 58 on spraying both sides with a nail board) and then let the sealer dry for about 2 to 3 hours.

6. **Sand the sealer** using a non-clogging (stearated) sandpaper. The sealer is dry enough to sand when it powders up nicely.

7. **Vacuum the sealer dust** and sandpaper debris with a vacuum.

Gun setup	
Gravity	1.3 mm–1.5 mm
Pressure cup	0.9 mm–1.0 mm
Siphon cup	1.7 mm–1.9 mm

Basic solvent-borne lacquer finish

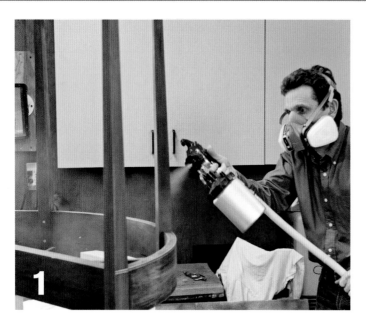

When the lacquer sanding sealer has dried according to the manufacturer's instructions (usually 2 to 4 hours) and it's been sanded and the dust removed, you can spray the clear lacquer topcoat in the sheen you like. Thin the lacquer 20 to 30 percent by volume with lacquer thinner. If the manufacturer says not to thin, you can spray the finish unthinned, but you may have to increase the nozzle size from the recommendations given.

1. **The base** is sprayed the same way you spray the sealer. Prop it up on riser blocks and work from the inside (least visible) areas to the outside (most visible).

2. **Do the most critical surfaces last.** Pick the base up in an area where there's no finish. After spraying it, move it aside.

3. **Spray one coat of clear lacquer topcoat** on the non-show side of the top and flip it over on the nail board and spray one coat on the show side.

4. **Let the lacquer dry** about 1 to 2 hours (check the label to see when you can safely re-coat) and lightly scuff sand any imperfections with 400-grit non-clogging (stearated) sandpaper.

5. **You can build more coats** on the base and top. I typically spray three coats total on the top and two on the base. Before you spray your final coat, lightly sand any imperfections, if necessary, with 400-grit and vacuum the powder. Use a tack cloth to make sure all particles are removed and finally vacuum yourself.

6. **Spray the last coats** on the base and the top. Light the area well. (Note the backlighting in the photo.) Make sure you get the last coat on the top as perfect as you can, as that's what people see the most.

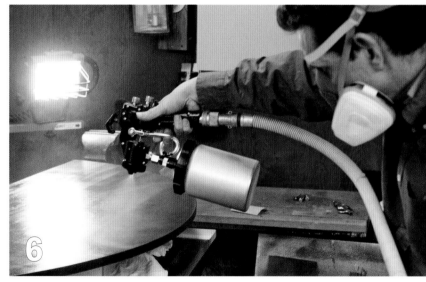

Gun set up	
Gravity	1.4 mm–1.7 mm
Pressure cup	0.9 mm–1.1 mm
Siphon cup	1.8 mm–2.0 mm

Spraying shellac

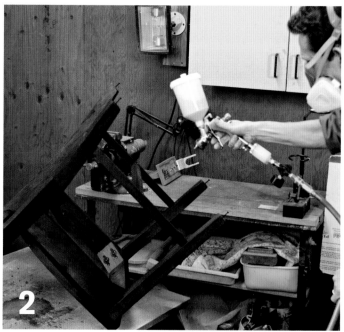

hellac makes a great sealer for the waterborne finish we'll be applying as the final finish on this chair. I have already sprayed the project with a waterborne stain (see p. 89). Make sure you take the correct precautions when you spray shellac. It's a flammable finish.

1. **Prop the piece off the platform** with screws when you spray a complicated project like this chair.

2. **Start with the undercarriage.** Spray the bottom of the seat and the inside legs and stretchers. I'm using a 3 in. fan-width pattern.

3. **Turn the chair over** and spray the legs, tops, and spindles, working from the bottom to the top.

4. **Change the fan width to a 6-in. pattern** before you do the top of the seat.

5. **Spray the seat last.** Add a few coats, as the seat gets the most wear.

Gun set up

Gravity	1.2 mm–1.4 mm
Pressure cup	0.7 mm–1.0 mm
Siphon cup	1.6 mm–1.8 mm

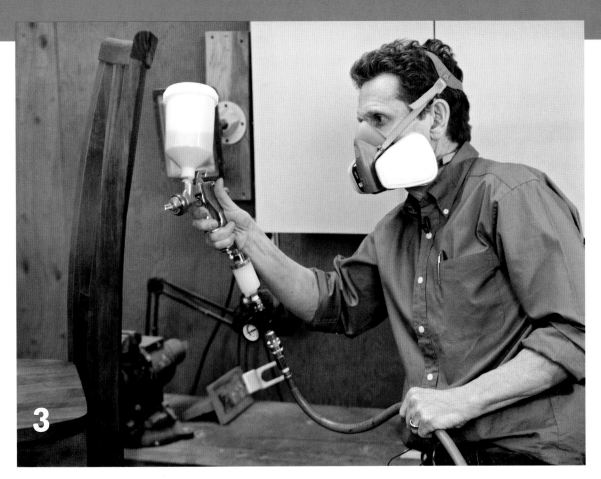

3

4

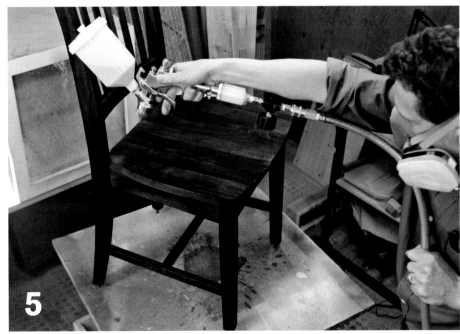

5

Spraying waterborne finish

The alcohol-based dewaxed shellac makes a great sealer for waterborne products. It dries fast, and doesn't raise the grain very much. But it isn't very durable, so I'll topcoat it with a waterborne varnish that should give plenty of protection to this chair.

1. **Sand the sealer,** after it has dried overnight, with 600-grit sandpaper to smooth it. (In this case, the sealer is a solvent-based dewaxed shellac.)

2. **Make sure the gun is clean** and free of any previously used finish. Because I had used the same gun the prior day to apply shellac, which cleans up with alcohol, I ran some water through the gun to flush out any remaining alcohol, which might cause problems with the waterborne finish I'm using.

3. **Apply the finish to the underside** first so that you can get the finish fluid flow and fan width adjusted.

4. **Spray the most visible parts last.** The main thing to watch out for is the tendency of waterborne finishes to drip on a vertical surface. I spray lighter coats on the spindles and legs.

5. **Apply a heavier coat to heavily used areas** like the seat because its flat and typically gets more wear and tear.

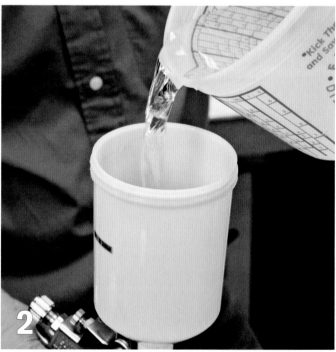

Gun setup

Gravity	1.5 mm–1.9 mm
Pressure cup	1.0 mm–1.3 mm
Siphon cup	1.9 mm–2.5 mm

3

4

5

Spraying paint

Spraying paint produces a superior finish free of brush marks, drips, sags, and puddles, and you can apply paint faster. You'll also find it easier to paint complicated and irregular surfaces like legs, moldings, and profiles.

Achieving a beautiful finish with paint requires a little more attention to thinning and proper gun setup. Paints sold for consumer use are designed for hand application and are purposely thickened so they don't spatter when rolled or drip when brushed. This heavy viscosity requires that you thin the paint correctly and use the correct nozzle.

Types of paints

Paints sold for home use fall into two classes: oil-based and waterborne. Oil-based paint goes by other names including "alkyd paint" or "oil-based enamel." Waterborne paints are generally referred to as latex paint, but you may also encounter terms such as "vinyl" or "acrylic." The main thing that separates these two is that oil-based paints thin and clean up with paint thinner or mineral spirits and waterborne paints thin and clean up with water.

Forty years ago, latex paint accounted for about 30 percent of total sales of paint. Today that number is about 80 percent. In certain areas of the country, oil-based paint may not even be available because of environmental concerns.

Oil-based paint formulations have a matrix or binder that holds the pigment particles together and

Like clear finishes, paints can be broadly grouped into oil-based (left) or waterborne paint. Waterborne paints are called latexes.

bonds them to wood. This is technically called an alkyd. Alkyds are synthetic products made by mixing reactive chemicals with plant oils such as tung, linseed, or soya. Today soya oil is mainly used. Colored pigment particles are ground into the alkyd and then mineral spirits are added to dilute it.

Specialty oil-based paints are available that are made with polyurethane or silicone binders to improve durability. Oil-based paints dry a little harder than waterborne paints and generally are easier to use on complex surfaces because they flow out better and are less prone to running and drips. They can be sprayed to a glass-smooth, flawless finish under a wide range of temperature and humidity conditions, except for high heat and humidity. However, they take a long time to dry before you can apply a second coat (usually 12 to 24 hours) and emit a strong solvent odor as they dry. They are also more prone to yellowing as they age.

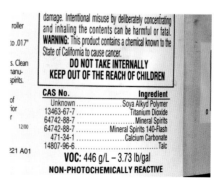

The three main ingredients in a typical oil-based paint are an alkyd binder, colored pigment (titanium dioxide is a white pigment), and mineral spirits.

These latex paints are all interior acrylic-based paints. They are suitable for applying to furniture or cabinets. "Bath and Kitchen" paints have a chemical added to inhibit mold growth in wet conditions.

Waterborne paints are loosely referred to as "latexes," but there are various binders used in waterborne paints and some are not suitable for use on furniture. Typical wall paint is based on a vinyl binder that's too soft and fragile for furniture. It's also prone to "blocking," which means that objects like books, vases, or plates left on the dried paint will stick to it. When you paint furniture or cabinets you want paint that contains 100 percent acrylic as the binder. These paints are usually known as interior latex trim enamels, acrylic enamels, or acrylic latex enamel. Always look for both terms "interior use" and "100% acrylic" in the description to differentiate it from lower-quality wall paint. Waterborne acrylics dry much faster than oil paints and can be re-coated in 2 to 4 hours. They have much less of an odor and typically do not have a lingering solvent smell after

If you see the term "vinyl" in the list of ingredients, it's a wall paint. Don't use it on furniture.

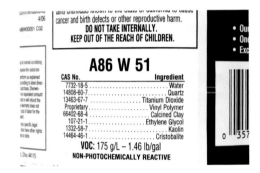

When looking for a furniture-grade latex paint, look for the term "acrylic resin" or "polymer" in the list of ingredients.

Tinted waterborne finishes

Some manufacturers make spray-only waterborne acrylic lacquers and polyurethanes which are not thickened, so you do not have to thin them. You won't find these at home centers and hardware stores. They are available through distributors selling to professionals and small cabinet shops as well as from some mail order retailers.

Primers fall into one of three basic types. From left: oil based, shellac based and latex (waterborne).

1 to 2 days like oil-based products. They are less prone to yellowing. On the downside, they can be difficult to apply in extremes of cold and heat and generally do not flow out to a glass-like surface the way oil-based paints do, particularly in gloss.

Surface preparation

On new wood, surface preparation is the same as for natural or stained wood, except that you only have to sand to 150-grit. The paint will fill in any minor sanding marks so higher grits like 180 or 220 aren't necessary. Fill all imperfections such as cracks, checks, dents, knots, and joinery gaps with putty after sanding. If you miss something that's OK, you can fix it after the first coat of primer. I prefer water-based filler because it dries fast and sands easily and it works just as well under oil-based paint as it does under latex. Finally, lightly sand the edges on all the parts with 150-grit because the paint won't stick to a sharp edge. Then remove all the sanding dust with a vacuum.

Primers

A primer provides a base for the paint. It functions primarily as an easy-to-sand sealer, but primers have other purposes in paint applications. Most primers contain a chalk-like mineral that fills microscopic voids and grain in the wood that would show when the paint is applied.

White primer really shows imperfections after the first coat. You can putty over the primer as long as you sand it before applying another coat.

Sanding all the sharp edges before painting is one of the keys to a great painted finish.

If you need to tint the primer to a darker color for use with a dark paint, use a colorant called a UTC (Universal Tinting Colorant). This universal tint will work with all three types of primer.

Primer also does a better job of sealing end grain than paint. Since paint accentuates minor imperfections and grain much more than a clear finish, primers become important elements in a good paint finish. Primers can also solve problems like paint discoloration from high-tannin woods and knot-bleed in pines, or provide better grip to previously finished surfaces. Most major manufacturers carry several different primers.

Shellac-based primers are good all-around primers, particularly if you are unsure about which one to use.

Shellac primers are made from clear dewaxed shellac, white pigment, and mineral fillers. The most common brand you'll find is B-I-N® primer by the Wm Zinsser Company. Shellac primers are absolutely the best for sealing in pitch and knots in pine and other species containing resinous knots. Shellac primer also has tremendous adhesion to old surfaces and is used to insure that a new paint will adhere to a previously finished surface. It can be used to insure adhesion to manufactured products like chipboard, hardboard, and plastic. Downsides are its flammability, and it doesn't sand as well as the other primers.

Latex primers are general purpose and can be used satisfactorily as primers on most new wood finishes. If you have a high-tannin wood like oak, cedar, or birch you

workSmart

One trick I've used many times is to spot seal knots and resinous areas with shellac primer. I let it dry , then I prime the rest of the project with a primer that sands more easily.

Latex primers (also known as undercoaters) dry fast, have low odor, and sand easily. The main disadvantage is that they raise the grain.

Oil-based (alkyd) primers can be used under both oil and water-borne paints. They brush easily and are a good choice when you don't want to raise the grain, but they dry more slowly.

want to make sure that the primer has a tannin block, which prevents discoloration in the primer and paint. If you're not sure, use shellac- or oil-based primer. Latex primers sand very easily.

Oil (alkyd) primers are good all-purpose primers. They can be used with both oil and latex paints, but they dry more slowly than other primers. Oil primers are effective against tannin bleed but not as effective on pitch and knots as shellac-based primers. However, they don't raise the grain so you save sanding time. Oil-based primers can be used with either oil or latex paints, but check with the manufacturer of the paint just to be sure. Oil primers sand very well.

If you're unsure about which primer to use, use shellac-based primer. It solves just about every potential problem, has minimal grain raising, and costs about the same as the others.

Patching and puttying

After bare wood sanding, patch the visible gaps, holes, dents, and other areas with latex wood filler. If the holes are large and deep like knots, use a non-shrinking filler or plan to apply a second fill after the first dries. After your first putty application, sand with 150-grit sandpaper and then apply your first primer coat. When it dries, you'll probably see other imperfections that weren't visible before. Apply wood filler or a lightweight spackle compound using just the tip or corner of the putty knife and sand with 220-grit sandpaper before applying another primer coat.

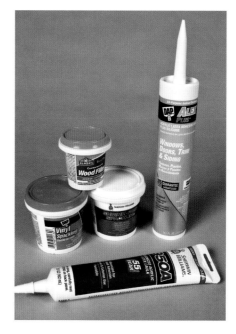

Most of the putties and wood fillers you'll find are latex (waterborne) based, and they can be used under any type of paint. Caulks are used where you have large gaps, like where crown molding meets the ceiling on a built-in cabinet.

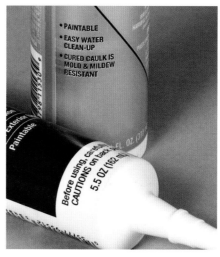

Make sure the caulk states "paintable" somewhere on the tube.

Most consumer-grade paints available in home centers and hardware stores will have to be thinned to apply with a spray gun.

Patching and puttying in this two-step method insures as flawless a surface as possible. If you do see a small problem after the first coat of paint, you can let it dry and apply a fast-dry spackle (I like a product called DAP®), let it dry, and sand it carefully before applying the final coats.

If you are painting built-in cabinetry and you have large gaps to fill, such as between moldings and the wall or ceiling, use caulk instead of wood filler or spackle. It's more flexible and won't shrink back or fall out later.

Choosing and thinning paint

As mentioned, oil-based paints are unavailable in certain areas. Where allowed they are frequently used by architects and designers where a glass-like or porcelain-looking paint finish is required. Latex paints don't flow out quite as well, particularly in gloss sheens, so you may

Use VM&P Naphtha to thin oil paint. It's a better thinner for spraying.

want to use oil-based paint in these situations. Oil-based paints are also a good choice over old oil-based paint or for finishing over old clear finishes where you're unsure of what the old finish might be.

Latex paints are my personal paint of choice and I can get pretty close to an oil-based look. If you need to make sure the latex will stick to something previously finished, you can always use shellac primer. The main advantages to latex are ease of clean-up, they are safer to use (non-flammable), and low odor, all of which make them very desirable over oil-based paints.

When using oil-based paint for furniture or cabinets, it's best to use trim enamel instead of oil wall paint. While mineral spirits or paint thinner may be specified for the thinner, it's better to use solvent called VM&P (Varnish Makers & Painters) Naphtha, which is faster drying than mineral spirits. If you use regular mineral spirits or paint thinner, you may experience sags and runs. It's hard to pinpoint an exact amount for thinner, but typical trim enamel requires 10 to 15% naphtha by volume (3 oz. to 5 oz. per quart paint) and a 1.3 mm to 1.5 mm nozzle set-up for a pressure-feed gun or a 1.9 mm. to 2.2 mm nozzle setup for a gravity-feed gun. I typically fill up a quart paint cup to the 28 oz. mark and then add 4 oz. of naphtha. Try spraying this mix with a 1.3 mm nozzle. If it sputters and spits, you can either move to a larger size nozzle or add more thinner until it atomizes well. Try not to exceed 6 oz. of naphtha per quart of finish if possible.

I get the best results using the following procedure to thin a latex enamel for spraying. In a 1-qt. paint mixing cup put 3 oz. distilled water. Add 3 oz. of Floetrol®, a product made specifically for latex paint to help it flow out better. Then fill to the 32 oz. mark with your paint and stir for 1 minute. Use a 1.5 mm nozzle setup for a pressure feed gun and a 2.2 mm to 2.5 mm nozzle for a gravity gun.

warning

Don't even try to spray latex in an HVLP gun without thinning it first. It won't work. But if you plan to spray large exterior projects like a house or interior walls, you may want to consider renting an airless spray rig. These pumps can handle large 5-gal. pails of latex with no thinning required.

The basics of spraying paint

To get a flawless paint finish make sure you follow the previous steps regarding surface preparation, which is 75 percent of the work you'll put into the finish. Of course, if you're after a less sophisticated or rustic effect you can simply apply the paint to the bare wood, which shows the minor imperfections and grain.

After thinning the paint, strain it into your spray gun cup through a medium-mesh paper paint strainer. When spraying the paint, practice on a piece of cardboard or a

A 2.5 mm nozzle that's installed in this gravity gun is much larger than ones used for clear finishes. A 1.6 mm is held next to it for comparison. Don't even try to spray latex with a small nozzle.

Getting the right atomization

An easy way to check proper atomization of colored paint is to spray it on a piece of white paper. The pattern at the bottom is under-atomized and won't flow out well. Aim for a pattern that looks like the top one. On a spray system where you can't control the air (a turbine), you'll have to thin a little more or change the nozzle size.

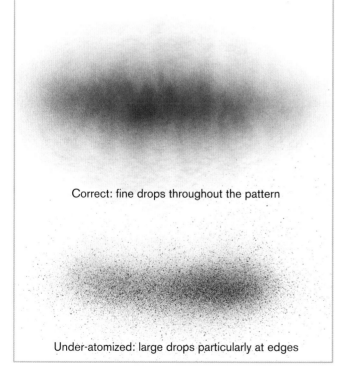

Correct: fine drops throughout the pattern

Under-atomized: large drops particularly at edges

practice board to make sure the paint is atomizing properly and you have the correct settings. One trick to see if the paint is atomizing properly is to turn the fan width control up to the widest setting you'll use and spray a quick pass on a sheet of cardboard. Insufficient air shows up as large drops on the outside edges of the pattern.

When spraying the first coats of primer and paint, turn down the air atomization so they can get into all the grooves, details, and corners, otherwise you'll be tempted to lay down too heavy a coat, which will run. Turning down the air lowers the vortex created by the atomized paint pattern and allows the paint to get into the corners better.

Once all the complicated areas have been covered, turn the air atomization up to normal to complete the coat. With the initial coats of primer, always "double-pass" the end grain areas, meaning spray all the end grain once, move on to spraying the rest of the piece, then spray the end grain again. The two coats compensate for initial primer coats soaking into the end grain. When spraying oil-based paint, I typically apply the coats at the end of the day to avoid kicking up dust and debris, which inevitably lands in the slow-drying finish.

To improve the durability of a latex finish, an optional step is to apply two coats of a clear, non-yellowing waterborne finish after the paint has dried 1 to 2 days. You can also do this if you're unsure about the blocking resistance of the latex. To insure adhesion, sand the dried paint with a gray abrasive pad like ScotchBrite®. You can also do this if you're after a glossy or flat finish, as many latex trim enamels do not come in these sheens.

Thinning latex paint

Manufacturers of latex paint generally advise to thin latex paint no more than 10 percent, which is equal to about 3 oz. of water per quart. I've thinned latex as high as 15 percent (5 oz.) with no problems, but keep in mind the more water you add, the more likely the paint will run on a vertical surface. While I've used tap water with no apparent ill effects, it's advisable to use distilled water to avoid possible problems. If you have well water you should definitely use distilled water.

1. **Assemble your mixing kit:** a 1-qt. mixing cup, filters, distilled water, and Floetrol (an additive designed to help paint flow out better; it should be available wherever you buy your paint).

2. **Add 3 oz. of distilled water** to a 1-quart mixing pail.

3. **Add 3 oz. of Floetrol.** Stir for about 10 seconds.

4. **Fill the pail to the 32 oz. mark** with your latex paint and stir for about 1 minute.

5. **Strain this mixture into your spray gun cup.** Do not use any internal strainers (the kind that fit inside the cup) with latex, as they are usually too fine to let the paint through.

Priming with shellac

Shellac primer is a good choice for this pine bookcase because of the knots. Latex primer would raise the grain, requiring a lot of extra sanding after it's applied. I'm thinning it about 10 percent because I want a light first coat to act as a base for the first round of patching.

1. **Thin the shellac primer** only with denatured alcohol. Use a ratio of 1 oz. alcohol to 10 oz. of shellac that I poured into the mixing cup.

2. **Stir the mix for about 30 seconds** and then strain it into your cup using a medium-mesh strainer.

3. **Remove the back,** if possible, and finish it separately. Finish the least visible side first, which will also allow you to adjust your gun settings.

4. **Finish the underside** and hard-to-get-at places first.

5. **Use riser blocks to raise the piece** off the platform. In this case, it allows me to spray the bottom of the legs. While the shellac dries fast, I really don't worry if the blocks mark the bottom of the fresh shellac.

6. **Turn down the atomizing air** from 30 psi to 20 psi for a softer spray to get into the reveals and the corners inside of the bookcase.

(continued on p. 84)

Gun setup	
Gravity	1.6 mm–1.9 mm
Pressure cup	1.1 mm–1.3 mm
Siphon cup	1.9 mm–2.2 mm

3

4

5

6

7. **Turn up the atomizing air** to spray the larger open areas. Spray all the end grain areas with one quick pass. Then move on to the rest of the case. Spray the inside then the outside, then give the end grain one more pass.

8. **Spray the shelves** that have previously been removed. Use a nail board to eliminate any marks. (See "Spraying both sides with a nail board," on p. 58.)

Filling imperfections

Try to patch as many imperfections as possible with putty before spraying your first primer coat. After the first primer has dried, go over the surface again and use putty on the minor imperfections that are bound to show. I use latex putty with both oil and latex paints because it dries faster.

1. **Do a last check** for imperfections. I missed the knot squarely in the center of the top rail. Note how the white primer makes it really visible.

2. **Use a wood filler** to fill the imperfection. One this deep might take two applications.

3. **To fill smaller areas,** try to put the filler exactly where it's needed using the tip of the putty knife. This eliminates a lot of sanding later.

4. **Sand the filler flush** with 240-grit sandpaper after the filler has thoroughly dried. Then sand the rest of the cabinet to remove the roughness from the first coat of primer. Remove the dust and apply one more coat of primer.

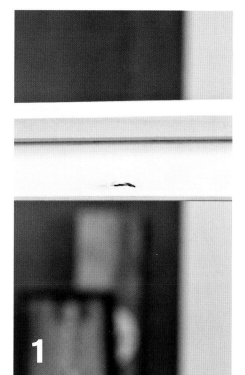

Spraying latex paint

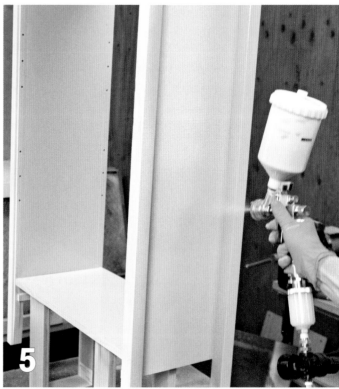

Make sure you follow the procedure for thinning latex paint (on p. 78) and practice to make sure your pattern is correct. The hardest parts are the verticals, where you may get runs and drips if the coat is too heavy. To spray the sides, you can always lay the project on its side.

1. **Sand the dry primer** with 320-grit sandpaper to remove any roughness and to smooth the primer. Make sure the sandpaper you use is compatible with water-based finishes.

2. **Use a tack rag** (one that's rated for use with waterbornes) to remove the fine dust from sanding.

3. **Adjust the fan width control** for a small fan width and fluid delivery. Turn the atomizing pressure down 25 to 33 percent from the normal position and spray all the inside corners and profiles.

4. **Spray the inside,** the outside corners, and profiles.

5. **Adjust the air pressure** back to normal and increase the fan width and fluid delivery. Spray the insides and the outsides. You can turn the aircap 90 degrees to do the long sides.

6. **Spray the most critical areas,** or the ones that are most visible next. In this case it's the bottom and the face frame.

7. **Spray the top last.**

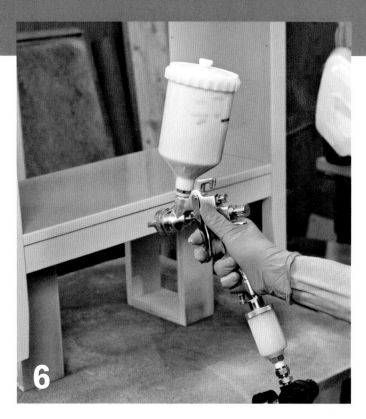

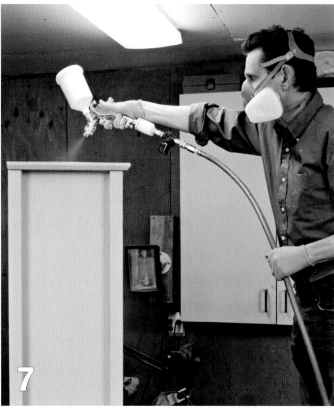

Gun setup

Gravity	2.2 mm–2.5 mm
Pressure cup	1.5 mm–1.8 mm
Siphon cup	not recommended

Special techniques

Besides spraying clear finishes and paint, a spray gun can apply products like stains and toners. Applying a stain with a spray gun will speed up the application process, particularly on large or complicated items. There are even techniques for applying stains that don't have to be wiped after application (like dyes), which results in a more uniform color. A spray gun can also apply lightly tinted finishes (called toners) to produce specific effects or to solve problems.

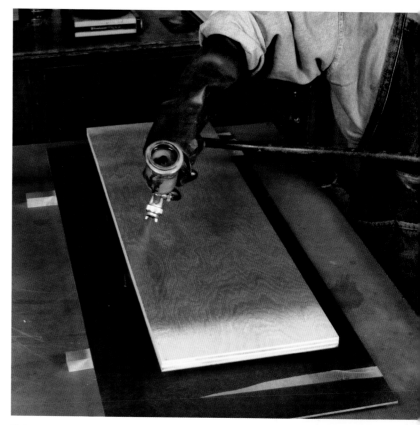

Using a spray gun to apply stain will speed up the process, particularly if you have to stain a lot of pieces or a complicated project.

Spraying stains

Spraying stains is much faster, particularly for complicated or large surfaces. Most stains must be wiped after spray application, which is why they are called "wiping stains." The oil-based and waterborne wiping stains available at home centers and hardware stores belong in this category.

Stains that don't have to be wiped after application are dye-based stains. They are sold as pre-mixed NGR (non-grain raising) stains or as liquids or powders that the user mixes with water or alcohol. These "no-wipe" stains have a big benefit. Not wiping the stain results in more even stain coverage on woods like pine and cherry. These species often stain unevenly (called splotching).

Wiping stains and dye stains are much thinner than finishes, so use the chart on p. 90 as a starting point for setting up your gun.

These stains are meant to be wiped after application. If you don't wipe them, you risk problems with the finish adhering or drying correctly.

When spraying a fast-dry stain, work on a manageable area, then wipe it before it starts to set. If it sets before you can wipe it, try spraying over it to re-wet the first application.

Tape off areas that you don't want stained, like the sides and interior of this drawer.

Spraying a no-wipe stain like this water-soluble dye is a great way to handle uneven staining (splotching).

Wiping stains

When you spray a wiping stain be sure to mix it thoroughly before spraying so you disperse any color that has settled to the bottom of the container. Oil-based stains typically have enough open time that you can usually apply the stain over the entire surface and then wipe it afterwards. When I spray a faster-drying water-based wiping stain on large surfaces, I usually wear a painters mitt in my free hand so that I can wipe the stain before it starts to set. Apply the stain on each part or area (sides, tops, insides, etc.) and wipe it before moving on to the next part or area. On smaller items, you can apply the stain to the entire surface, then wipe it.

No-wipe stains

Spraying a no-wipe stain prevents the uneven distribution of color called "splotching." Woods that stain unevenly include pines and firs, cherry, birch, poplar, and some maples. You can also get a very pronounced light/dark effect when you stain raised-panel doors, turned legs, or other parts that have alternating end and face grain.

Gun setup for stains

	WIPING STAINS	DYE STAINS
Gravity feed	1.3 mm–1.5 mm	0.8 mm–1.2 mm
Siphon feed	1.6 mm–1.8 mm	1.4 mm–1.5 mm
Pressure feed	1.0 mm	0.5 mm–1.0 mm

A toner can solve finishing problems. On this cherry table a toner is being sprayed to even out and darken the color.

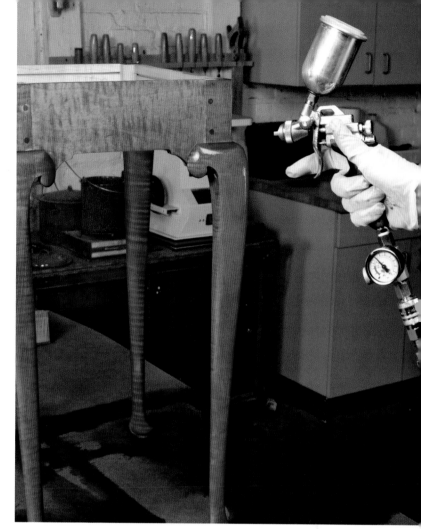

A no-wipe stain minimizes the light/dark effect that occurs in highly figured wood where the grain changes direction.

Toners

A toner is basically a clear finish mixed with color. Toners are used for a variety of effects by finishing professionals. In a small shop, toners are especially useful to changing the color of a piece that has already been sealed or finished. For example, you stain and finish a project and then decide later that you'd like it to be darker. Toner allows you to change the color without stripping the finish and starting over.

A toner can also be used to darken areas that are lighter than others, such as sapwood. While some sap areas are very visible and can be addressed in the initial staining stage, sometimes sapwood is difficult to detect and only becomes apparent as you start to finish.

Check the atomization

It's very important that you get good atomization when spraying a no-wipe stain. Test your atomization by spraying some of the dye onto white paper first.

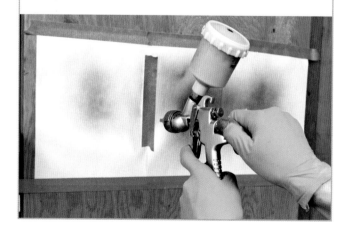

This cherry table base shows the subtle effects you can get with toner. A reddish-brown toner has been applied to the base. The drawer front hasn't been toned yet.

Sometimes sapwood isn't really apparent until you start finishing. A toner solves this problem easily.

Making a toner

Toners are not sold as such, but they're easy to make yourself. You can add color to any type of clear finish. My favorite is dewaxed shellac. Dewaxed shellac sprays very easily with any gun used for clear finishes, so you don't need a special nozzle setup. You can buy dewaxed shellac premixed as SealCoat® or mix it yourself from dry shellac flakes. The premixed product is much easier to use. There are two kinds of colors you can add to the shellac, universal tinting colorants (known as UTC's), or alcohol-compatible dyes.

workSmart

If you don't want to use shellac, you can make a toner by adding one of the colorants above to a clear finish, as long as the finish and colorant are compatible. For example, if you are putting on the final clear coats and you want a little bit more red to the finish, you can add some red colorant to the topcoat.

You can make a toner from any clear finish and a compatible colorant. Liquid dye concentrates (available at specialty woodworking stores and some paint stores) make great transparent toners when mixed with shellac.

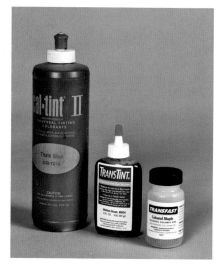

From left to right: Universal colorants are pigment-based colorants that can be added to any finish. Liquid dye concentrate can be added to all finishes except oil-based; dye powder can only be added to alcohol-based shellac.

Alcohol-compatible dyes are available as a powder or in liquid form. The liquid type is easier to use. Add the colorant to the shellac in small amounts, checking the result on a wooden stir stick.

Spraying a toner

While you can use any type of gun to spray a toner, my favorite by far is an inexpensive gravity detail gun. Detail guns come with smaller nozzles, so they atomize the toner very well.

Use a 1.0 mm to 1.2 mm nozzle setup in the gun to apply toner. After filling the cup through a strainer, adjust the spray pattern and atomizing air by spraying tests on white paper.

Toning techniques

There are two types of toning techniques, overall toning, and selective toning (also called shading).

Overall toning evenly changes the base color. It's used to make something darker or to change the hue, such as making something redder or more yellow. For overall toning, set the gun for a wide fan pattern.

Selective toning is used to add color to selected areas. Darkening sapwood or highlighting edges are examples of selective toning or shading.

Types of toning

Overall toning (bottom) evenly adds color, while selective toning (top) adds contrast and highlights.

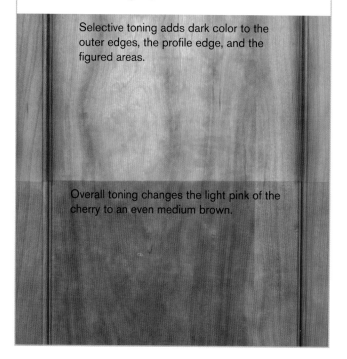

Selective toning adds dark color to the outer edges, the profile edge, and the figured areas.

Overall toning changes the light pink of the cherry to an even medium brown.

Spraying a wiping stain

This chair is a perfect project for spraying a wiping stain because there are so many surfaces and hard-to-reach areas. For a rich look, I'm using a dark walnut wiping stain.

1. **Put drywall screws on the bottom of the legs** to raise it above the spray platform.

2. **Starting on the undercarriage,** spray the bottom of the seat and the insides of all the legs and stretchers. Spray the bottom of the crest rail and other areas that would be hard to get at with the spray gun when the chair is turned upright. Wipe off excess stain from the underside before you turn the chair over.

3. **Spray all the spindles,** outsides of the legs, and stretcher tops, working your way from the bottom up.

4. **Spray the top of the crest rail.**

5. **Spray the seat last.**

6. **Wipe off any excess stain** while it's still wet.

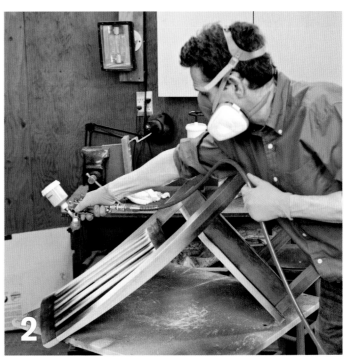

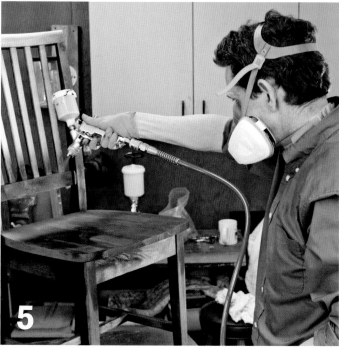

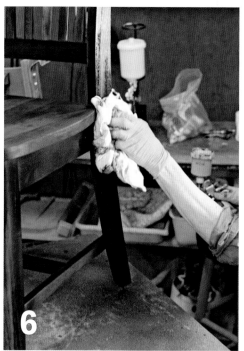

Spraying a no-wipe dye stain

This soft maple table is a great candidate for a no-wipe dye stain because of all the changing grain patterns, and soft maples tend to splotch. Make sure you have a fine atomized pattern by spraying some white paper or a practice piece first. I'm using a water-based dye made from a liquid concentrate.

1. **Start with the inside of the base.** Adjust the spray delivery so you have about a 4-in.-wide fan pattern. Cut back on the fluid so you have an almost misty pattern. When you spray, look for even, wet coverage but avoid getting it so wet that it drips.

2. **Turn the base upright and continue to spray** around the legs and aprons. As the stain dries it will look "dry" on areas you sprayed first. This is normal.

3. **Blot up the excess with an absorbent cloth,** if you get the stain a little on the wet side.

4. **Spray the underside of the top** and place it on a nail board. This highly profiled edge treatment requires that you make sure the dye gets into the crevices, so you may want to lower the atomizing air when you do the edges.

5. **Work from above** to spray the inside of the raised edge where it meets the top, and then the field.

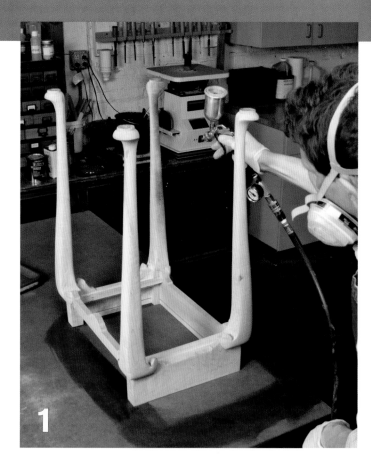

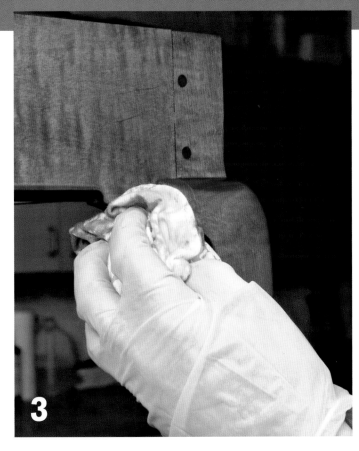

3

4

5

Making a toner

My favorite toner is made with dewaxed shellac, a liquid dye concentrate, and some denatured alcohol to thin the shellac. Using dewaxed shellac insures that the toner is compatible with any type of finish topcoat.

1. **Make a 1-lb.-cut shellac** by diluting 2-lb.-cut Seal-Coat with denatured alcohol in a mixing cup. Add the dye concentrate a little at a time while stirring.

2. **Check the concentration periodically** by looking at the paint stick. It's best to err on the slightly light side than your final color, that way you can build to the color you want in light coats rather than one heavy coat.

3. **Strain the mix** into your spray gun cup.

4. **Check the fan width controls** and atomizing air on a piece of white paper for a finely atomized pattern.

4

Overall toning

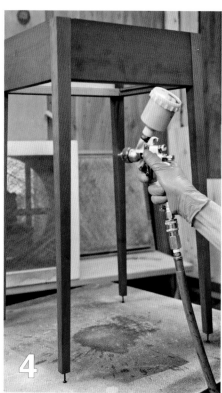

This unstained cherry nightstand looked great to me after two coats of clear finish. Then I decided I wanted it a little darker so it blended with some of the older cherry furniture I had. I'm using the toner described on pp. 98–99.

1. **Adjust the fan width** for a 2-in.-wide spray pattern and just a little fluid delivery. It's best to start on the light side and make adjustments after you get the feel for the technique. You can always go darker, but you can't wipe this toner off to make it lighter. Start on the insides of the four legs.

2. **Work on a turntable** so you can swivel the piece, which makes for a more evenly controlled spray.

3. **Adjust the fan width** for a larger 4-in. pattern for the rest of the toning.

4. **Spray the outside of larger surfaces,** such as the aprons and the outsides of the legs.

5. **Spray the frame** around the drawer.

6. **Make one complete pass on all areas,** and another if you want it darker. Remember to work from light to dark. Here's the untoned drawer installed just to show you the difference between the toned and untoned areas.

7. **Spray the top and the drawer separately.** On the drawer, mask off the areas where you don't want color.

Selective toning

The cherry nightstand looked pretty good from the previous step, but there were a few areas that needed some work. Working with a much darker toner than the one I used previously, I added some striking effects and addressed some lingering problems. These are the same techniques you'll see on factory furniture and musical instruments.

1. **Make a toner** that's darker than the dominant color in the wood. In this case I used the leftover toner from the toning step. I added a dark walnut concentrated dye to get this dark color.

2. **Shade the edges** of the legs and the base.

3. **Spray the top.** On this project, I used the dark toner to darken the lighter area on the top.

4. **Adjust the color** of any visible sapwood.

5. **Shade just the edges of the drawer** with the dark toner, circling around the perimeter.

6. **The completed table** shows the effect of the dark selective toning.

Cleanup and troubleshooting

C onsistently good results with spray finishing means knowing how to troubleshoot the problems that come up. Most of the time performance problems can be traced to improper cleaning or maintenance of the gun. You may also experience problems with the finish. These can usually be traced to spraying in temperature extremes (too hot or too cold) or improper technique (excessive overspray or dry spray). This chapter is about solving spray finishing problems.

Proper cleaning after you spray something like latex paint is essential if you want the spray gun to work properly the next time.

Cleaning up

Keeping your gun clean will ensure that it will work correctly the next time you use it. Sometimes it's good enough to just run some cleanup solvent through the gun, but for best performance you'll have to clean the gun more diligently.

It's important to remember that different finishes require different solvents and different schedules for cleanup. In some cases, they also have different techniques. Spraying different finishing materials back to back almost always entails using different cleanup solvents as well. Note that some products require a different cleaner once they have dried. (See the charts on the following pages.)

To clean your gun properly you'll need to invest in a spray gun cleaning kit. These kits contain the special brushes and cleaning needles to clean the small air and fluid passages in your spray gun.

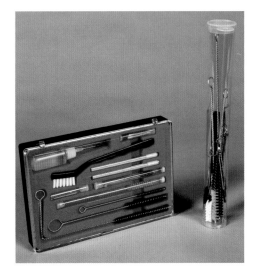

Spray gun cleaning kits have all the essential tools you need to keep your spray gun clean. The larger kit on the left has more specialized tools.

Cleanup solvents for finishes

	TO RINSE/CLEAN	TO REMOVE IF DRIED
Waterborne finishes, latex paint	Water followed by denatured alcohol	Acetone, lacquer thinner
Oil-based finishes, oil paint	Mineral spirits, paint thinner, naphtha	Lacquer thinner
Shellac	Denatured alcohol	Denatured alcohol
Solvent-based lacquer	Lacquer thinner	Lacquer thinner

Leaving finish in the gun

Since most sessions with fast-drying finishes are only a few hours apart, leaving finish in the gun doesn't cause problems. If you change to a different kind of finish or if you spray something that requires waiting until the next day to re-coat, you should always clean the gun. Don't leave finish in the gun overnight or longer.

If you leave waterborne finishes in the gun even for a few hours, a little "scab" will form around the fluid nozzle. The gun will spray erratically if you don't remove it. Just pry it off with a metal cleaning needle or a toothpick.

Cleaning between finishes

If you are changing finishing products that use the same cleanup solvent (like mineral spirits), you can simply pour the finish back into it's container and then run an ounce or two of cleanup solvent through the gun. That

should clean it enough to switch, unless the finish you've sprayed has color. Then you may need more solvent.

If you are switching finishes that use a different cleanup solvent, the procedure is more complicated. Some cleanup solvents do not mix with each other or don't rinse the gun's fluid passages well. Refer to the chart on the facing page for the correct solvent sequence when switching finishes.

Recycling solvents

Once you use a solvent for cleaning, you shouldn't use it for thinning. I keep it in a separate container that's properly labeled and reuse it only for cleaning. You can clean it by straining it or letting it sit for an hour and decanting the clear solvent that's at the top.

If you leave finish in the gun for a few hours, you may find that the gun won't spray at all or the pattern is wrong. The first thing to check is the tip of the fluid nozzle for any dried finish.

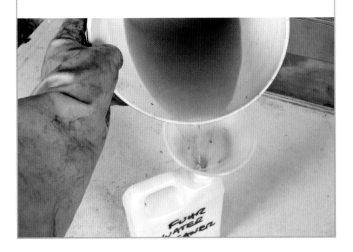

Cleanup at the end of the day

When you are done spraying you should run several ounces of cleanup solvent through the gun. The procedure is slightly different depending on whether you have a bottom feed (siphon) or top feed (gravity) gun.

Siphon guns First, remove the air line from the gun. Remove the gun and lid assembly from the cup, and holding the fluid pickup tube over the cup, pull the trigger to allow finish to drain back into the cup, and then pour the finish back into its container. Fill the cup up about halfway with the cleanup solvent (see chart on the facing page). Swirl the solvent around.

Hook up the air line, and if possible turn down the atomizing air. Some turbines have air flow valves on the gun or hose. Others have a speed control. Point the nozzle of the gun into a solvent container and spray the cleanup solvent through the gun. Remove the aircap, fluid nozzle and needle and wipe these items clean with a solvent-dampened rag. Inspect the fluid nozzle for any finish and use a micro-cleaning brush or toothpick if necessary to clear it. Dip the end of a rag into some of the remaining solvent in the cup and wipe the outside of the air cap, cup, and gun body if necessary. Wipe inside the cup lid and any gaskets and splash guards. On a suction gun make sure the air vent in the top of the cup is clean.

Always keep cleanup solvent in a separate container. When using any solvent for cleaning it's important to keep your respirator on.

A micro-brush from a cleaning kit is the only way to clean dried finish inside the fluid nozzle.

workSmart

If you spray paint, you may have to change to a clean solvent after the first rinse to make sure you remove all the paint. If any paint dries on parts, use lacquer thinner to remove it, as the original cleanup solvent won't be strong enough.

Cleanup to switch finishes

The chart below shows you the proper sequence of solvents to use to switch from one type of finish to another. For example W/DA/MS means clean with water, then denatured alcohol, then mineral spirits.

	Switch to oil-based finishes & paint	Switch to shellac	Switch to solvent lacquer	Switch to waterborne finishes & paint
Waterborne finishes & latex paint	W/DA/MS	W/DA	W/DA/LT	W
Oil-based finishes & oil paint	MS	MS/DA	MS/LT	MS/DA/W
Shellac	DA/MS	DA	DA/LT	DA/W
Solvent lacquer	LT/MS	LT/DA	LT	LT/DA/W

W = Water   DA = Denatured alcohol   MS = Mineral spirits, paint thinner or Naphtha   LT = Lacquer thinner

A gravity gun allows you to fill the cup with solvent and just let it flow through the gun. You don't have to hook up the air to do this.

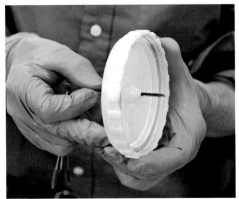

Whether it's a suction or gravity gun, always makes sure the vent in the cup lid is cleared of finish.

Gravity guns Remove the air line from the gun. Pour any remaining finish back into the container and then fill the cup halfway with solvent. Holding the gun above the solvent container, pull the trigger completely to allow solvent to flow through the fluid nozzle by gravity. Adjust the fluid needle for maximum fluid if necessary. Pour any remaining solvent back into a container and then remove the cup. Remove the aircap, fluid nozzle, and needle and wipe these items clean with a solvent-dampened rag. Inspect the fluid nozzle for any finish and use a micro-cleaning brush or toothpick if necessary to clear it. Dip the end of a rag into some of the remaining solvent in the cup and wipe the outside of the air cap, cup, and gun body if necessary. Wipe inside the cup lid and make sure you clear the air vent on the cup top.

Cleaning to solve atomization problems

If you experience atomization problems (poor patterns, the finish comes out too slow, parts stick), your gun needs a good cleaning. You should also do this on a regular basis as part of monthly preventative maintenance, especially if you use your gun frequently. You'll need a cleaning kit that has the necessary brushes and cleaning tools. You'll also need gun lubricant or petroleum jelly.

Cleaning all the micro-passages and fluid and air ports usually solves most atomization problems and is a great way to solve a problem that you can't otherwise

Some items you will need for cleanup, from left to right: The first four brush sets and brushes are used for aircap and nozzle cleaning. The next three brushes are for cleaning the fluid pickup tube. The black-handled bristle brush is used for cleaning cup threads and the outside of the gun, and the small metal pick on the far right is used to remove o-rings and gaskets. You can use either petroleum jelly or gun lube as lubricants.

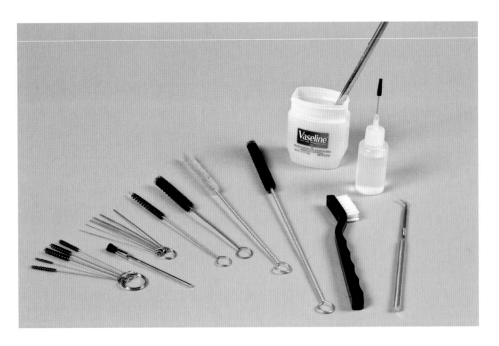

A magnifying glass allows you to see minor problems that cause misshaped patterns like in the drawing on the right.

diagnose. Once you give these parts a thorough cleaning, lubricate the gun (see p. 110). Then, spray some cleanup solvent through the gun to make sure it's working correctly.

see p. 110

Finally, test the gun with finish. Set the gun up for a medium to heavy fluid delivery and a medium to wide fan pattern. Spray some finish onto some cardboard until it starts to run. When you see the drips more or less evenly spaced, the gun is atomizing correctly. If you have a spray pattern that looks like one in the drawing at right, then remove and clean the aircap and fluid nozzle and make the suggested setup adjustments.

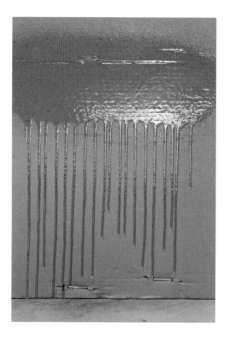

To test your pattern, turn the aircap for a horizontal pattern and spray finish on a piece of cardboard. A properly operating gun will have evenly spaced drips.

Troubleshooting atomization

1. 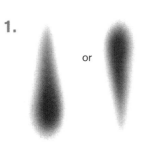 or

PROBLEM

Pattern top or center heavy

SOLUTION

Turn aircap 180 degrees. If problem reverses then air cap horn holes are obstructed. Clean aircap. If it doesn't reverse, clean fluid nozzle.

2. 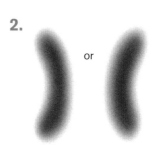 or

PROBLEM

Pattern curved

SOLUTION

One of the aircap holes on the horns is plugged. Clean.

3.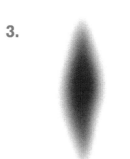

PROBLEM

Pattern is too heavy in the center

SOLUTION

Finish is too thick or atomization pressure is too low. Increase air pressure or thin material.

4.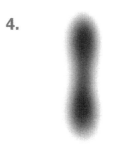

PROBLEM

"Split" spray pattern—center is starved

SOLUTION

Air pressure too high—reduce. Fluid tip is wrong size—check viscosity and change nozzle.

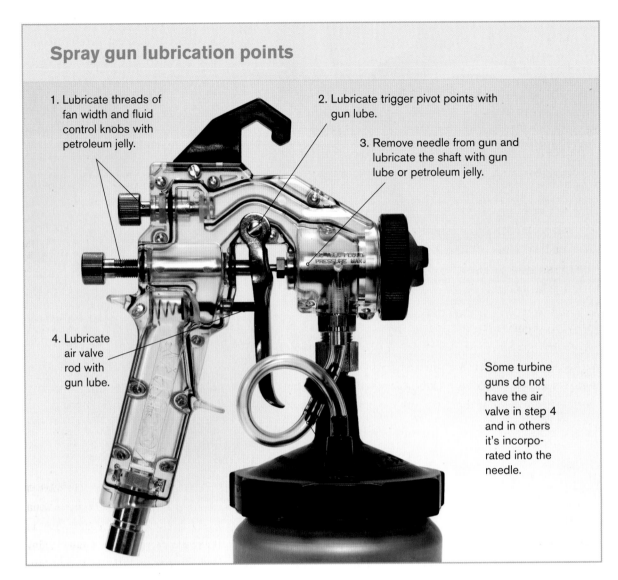

Spray gun lubrication points

1. Lubricate threads of fan width and fluid control knobs with petroleum jelly.

2. Lubricate trigger pivot points with gun lube.

3. Remove needle from gun and lubricate the shaft with gun lube or petroleum jelly.

4. Lubricate air valve rod with gun lube.

Some turbine guns do not have the air valve in step 4 and in others it's incorporated into the needle.

Blushing occurs when a fast-drying finish traps moisture, causing the finish to turn bone white.

Finish problems

Most problems with finishes are temperature or humidity related, which sometimes can be corrected with special additives for the specific finish. Or you may just have to wait until the weather improves.

Finish blush

Blushing shows up when shellac and solvent lacquer are sprayed in high humidity. The finish turns white shortly after you spray it, and it's alarming the first time you see it. The culprit is moisture from the air getting trapped into the surface of the fast-drying finish, turning it white. Stop spraying and try spraying some thinner on the surface (use denatured alcohol for shellac and lacquer thin-

Orange peel is a bumpy surface usually caused by too low an atomization air pressure.

Sometimes fish-eye looks a little like orange peel, but it's random. Note that the right side of the panel isn't affected.

ner for lacquer). The white should disappear. If it comes back you'll have to wait until the weather improves and sand the surface before spraying it with thinner. If it still doesn't go away, mix lacquer retarder into the lacquer thinner or denatured alcohol in the ratio of 1:10 parts retarder to thinner. The retarder keeps the thinner wet or active longer so it can remove the blush. The retarder can also be added directly to the lacquer or shellac if you need to spray on humid days. I try to avoid this if possible because it slows down the dry/cure time of the lacquer or shellac.

To remove fish-eye that's dried, sand the finish level with sandpaper.

Dry spray

Dry spray is a rough finish from overspray getting on a partially dry area or not getting enough finish on an area for it to flow and level out. You'll find it usually on insides of cabinets and around legs and stretchers and other complicated areas. You can smooth the roughness with very fine sandpaper (400 grit to 600 grit) and then re-spray if it's a prominent area. You can mask off surrounding areas to protect them from overspray. An alternative is to simply smooth the rough area with steel wool after it has dried several days.

Orange peel

Orange peel is a bumpy surface that you can see once the finish has dried. Follow these steps to correct the problem. First check your atomizing air pressure. When it's too low for the finish, you'll get orange peel because the finish doesn't get broken up enough. Try increasing the air pressure until the problem goes away. If it doesn't, try adding thinner in 5 percent increments. If that still doesn't work, try going to a smaller nozzle setup.

Fish-eye

Fish eye or "cratering" is a defect that sometimes looks like orange peel, except that fish-eye usually shows up as randomly spaced craters. The culprit is contamination from substances like oil that repel the finish as it starts to dry, causing it to form little craters or "eyes".

Fish-eye is difficult to deal with, but if you see it, wipe the finish off immediately. Clean the wood by scrubbing it with a scrub brush and lacquer thinner, using clean rags to remove the excess thinner. Then wash it down again with a clean rag dipped in thinner. If the fish-eye appears again, you'll either have to seal it in with dewaxed shellac after washing it down with lacquer thinner again, or add a fish-eye additive to your finish. Fish-eye additive is available for many professional solvent lacquer finishes and some varnishes. It is not available for waterborne products, so you'll have to seal the surface with dewaxed shellac.

The chart on pp. 112–113 has more information on dealing with finish and system performance problems.

Troubleshooting finishes

Problem	Cause	Remedy
AIR PROBLEMS		
Air leaking from pressurized cup	Dirty or worn cup gasket	Clean or replace
Air leaks at fittings	Fittings not tight	Tighten fittings or connections
	Fitting threads loose	Use Teflon tape on fittings
Air flows when trigger released (non-bleeder guns only)	Air valve plunger stuck	Clean and lubricate
FLUID/FINISH PROBLEMS		
Finish leaks at nozzle	Needle sticking in packing	Lubricate needle, loosen packing
	Compression spring missing or worn	Replace
	Needle tip damaged	Replace
	Nozzle damaged	Replace
Finish leaks at packing	Packing not sealing around needle	Tighten packing nut or replace packing
Finish leaks at cup	Cup gasket worn, missing, or dirty	Clean or replace
Gun won't spray finish	Finish not pulling up into gun (suction or gravity)	Clear air vents in cup lid and/or splashguard
	Check valve clogged (pressure cup feed)	Clean or replace
	Nozzle clogged	Clean
	Fluid pickup tube clogged (bottom-feed guns)	Clean
Fluttering/pulsating spray	Air leak	Tighten fluid nozzle, tighten aircap, tighten cup to gun
	Needle packing loose or worn	Tighten or replace
	Finish level low in cup or when gun tilted	Fill cup with finish
	Check valve partially obstructed (pressure feed)	Replace

Problem	Cause	Remedy
Fluttering/pulsating spray (continued)	Air Vent partially obstructed	Clean (gravity and suction feed)
	Material too thick	Thin material or use larger nozzle
	Fluid pickup tube partially clogged	Clean
Finish bubbles in cup (gravity only)	Air leak at fluid nozzle	Tighten fluid nozzle

SPRAY PATTERN PROBLEMS

Problem	Cause	Remedy
Pattern heavy on one side	(a) Aircap holes plugged on one side or damaged	Rotate aircap 180 degrees–if problem reverses, clean air cap holes; if not, go to (b)
(see drawing on p. 109)	(b) fluid tip damaged or clogged	Clean or replace fluid nozzle
Unable to achieve wide fan width	Finish too thick (suction feed)	Thin material
	Aircap air ports on side horns plugged	Soak aircap in lacquer thinner and clean
	Fan width control knob valve seat damaged	Replace
Coarse spray pattern (large droplets)	Too low air pressure	Increase air pressure
Too much overspray	Too high air pressure	Lower air pressure
Rough finish	Too high air pressure	Lower air pressure
	Gun too far away	Check proper gun distance
	Moving gun too fast	Slow down gun passes

Gun cleaning between different finishes

I used this gravity gun to apply an alcohol-based shellac sealer. Now I want to switch to a waterborne finish as the topcoat. I'll have to use two solvents to switch the gun over.

1. **Remove the air line** and pour the shellac finish back into its container. Fill the cup with denatured alcohol.

2. **Swirl the solvent** around in the cup.

3. **Holding the gun over the solvent container** pull the trigger completely, aiming the solvent back into the container. Adjust the fluid control knob until it's almost at the full limit of retraction. Run several ounces of solvent through the gun.

4. **Return the denatured alcohol to the container** and fill the cup with water (the thinner for waterborne).

5. **Run the water through the gun** the same way as the denatured alcohol. You can now fill the gun with the waterborne finish.

Gun cleaning at the end of the day

I'll use this turbine gun to demonstrate the basics of cleaning at the end of the spray session or if you are done for the day. You can also use this process for suction-feed guns.

1. **Remove the air hose** and remove the gun and lid assembly from the cup bottom. Hold the gun above the cup and pull the trigger to let excess finish in the fluid passage flow back into the cup.

2. **Pour the finish out** and fill the cup halfway with cleanup solvent. Hook the air hose back up and if possible turn down the air flow. With a compressor-driven gun, just reduce the atomizing air with the air regulator you use for the gun.

3. **Spray the cleanup solvent into the container** so you can reuse it. If it's water you can spray it outside.

4. **Return the solvent to its container.** Wipe the inside of the cup.

5. **Wipe the inside of the cup lid,** particularly around the gasket. Wipe the splashguard too (the white disc in the center of the cup).

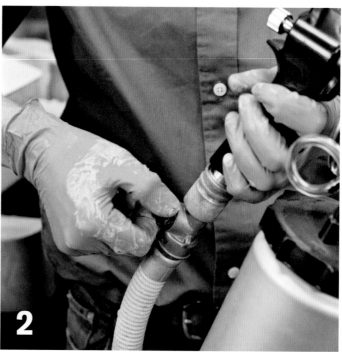

Problem solving and maintenance cleaning

If you have a problem that won't go away with a simple cleaning, try this more in-depth cleaning and lubrication routine. It's also good to do this if you're going to be storing your gun for a while.

1. **Remove the aircap retaining ring** and the aircap. On some guns, the retaining ring and aircap come off separately. On others, these parts are removed as an assembly.

2. **Remove the fluid control knob** by turning it counterclockwise. Remove the compression spring.

3. **Pull out the needle** from the back. If it's stuck, grab the back with needle-nose pliers.

4. **Put all three parts in some lacquer thinner** to soak. If they look dirty, you can also soak the fluid control knob and compression spring. Use micro-brushes to clean the finish passages on the gun body, and a large pickup-tube brush to clean the pickup tube. You may want to remove the gun from the cup assembly so the brush can be pushed all the way through the tube.

5. **Lay the parts out on a piece of cloth.**

6. **Inspect the holes in the aircap** and use micro-brushes from a spray gun cleaning kit to clean all the ports.

(continued on p. 120)

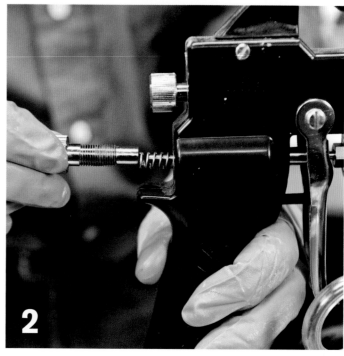

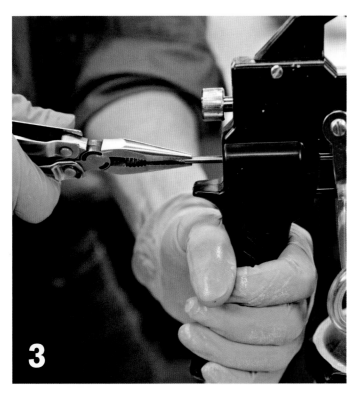

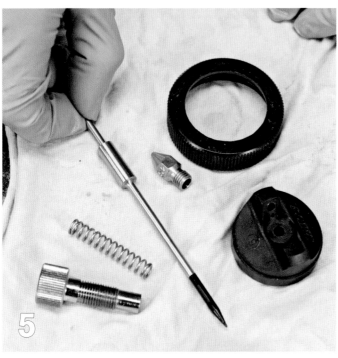

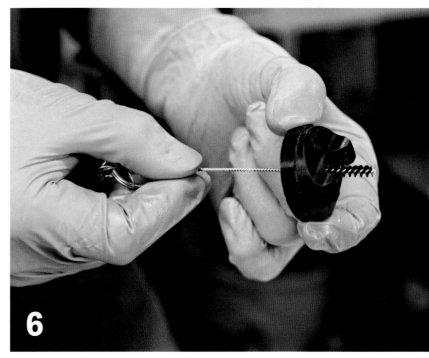

7. **Check the very small ports** around the center hole (on some low-cfm HVLP guns). These must be cleared with small wire cleaning needles.

8. **If finish has dried inside the fluid nozzle,** you'll see it come out the end when you push a micro-brush through from the back.

9. **Put the fluid nozzle back into the gun.**

10. **Check the needle for dried finish** and if you find any, remove it. Put some gun lube on the shaft of the needle where it slides back and forth inside the front end of the gun.

11. **Apply gun lube** or brush some petroleum jelly on the threads of the control knobs with a small brush.

12. **Replace the aircap,** add finish to the gun, and test the spray pattern on some cardboard.

workSmart

If you continue to have problems with your gun after cleaning it or trying the solutions given in the chart on pp. 112–113, you might have a damaged component or an internal seal or gasket that needs to be replaced. It's a good idea to contact the manufacturer before proceeding with major repairs unless you are mechanically inclined. Repair and rebuild kits are available through the manufacturer to replace the major wearable springs, gaskets, and seals for your spray gun.

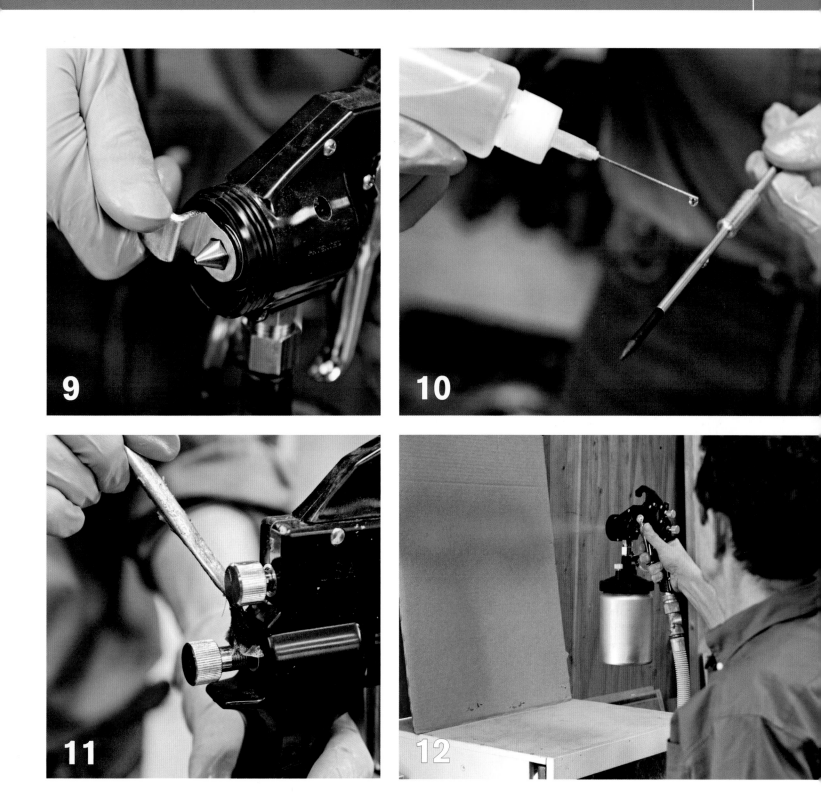

resources

A concerted effort was made throughout this book to use products easily available at most local home centers, paint, and hardware stores. For products not available in your local area, try these specific online companies.

For spray booth fans, commercial spray booths, and parts

- **Spray Shield Industries**
  888-883-4583
  www.sprayshield.com

For HVLP spray equipment and accessories

- **Homestead Finishing Products**
  866-631-5429
  www.homesteadfinishingproducts.com

- **Woodcraft®**
  800-535-4486
  www.woodcraft.com

- **Rockler℠ Woodworking and Hardware**
  800-279-4441
  www.rockler.com

Spray equipment manufacturers (consumer and industrial)

- **3M® Accuspray**
  877-666-2277
  www.solutions.3m.com

- **C.A. Technologies**
  888-820-4498
  www.spraycat.com

- **Fuji Industrial Spray Equipment Ltd.**
  800-650-0930
  www.fujispray.com

- **Apollo Sprayers® International, Inc.**
  888-900-4857
  www.hvlp.com

Spray Finishes (consumer and Industrial)

- **H Behlen Brothers**
  (water and solvent based)
  866-785-7781
  www.hbehlen.com

- **Hood® Finishing Products**
  (water and solvent based)
  800-229-0934
  www.hoodfinishing.com

- **Target Coatings®**
  (waterborne only)
  800-752-9922
  www.targetcoatings.com

- **General Finishes®**
  (water and solvent based)
  800-783-6050
  www.generalfinishes.com

index